Y0-ABI-174

Sustaining the Hope for Unity

Erin M. Brigham

SUSTAINING
THE HOPE FOR UNITY

Ecumenical Dialogue
in a Postmodern World

A Michael Glazier Book

LITURGICAL PRESS
Collegeville, Minnesota

www.litpress.org

A Michael Glazier Book published by Liturgical Press

Cover design by David Manahan, OSB. Photo courtesy of Thinkstock/iStockphoto.

Excerpts from documents of the Second Vatican Council are from *Vatican Council II: Volume 1, The Conciliar and Post Conciliar Documents*, by Austin Flannery, OP © 1996 (Costello Publishing Company, Inc.). Used with permission.

© 2012 by Order of Saint Benedict, Collegeville, Minnesota. All rights reserved. No part of this book may be reproduced in any form, by print, microfilm, microfiche, mechanical recording, photocopying, translation, or by any other means, known or yet unknown, for any purpose except brief quotations in reviews, without the previous written permission of Liturgical Press, Saint John's Abbey, PO Box 7500, Collegeville, Minnesota 56321-7500. Printed in the United States of America.

1   2   3   4   5   6   7   8   9

Library of Congress Cataloging-in-Publication Data

Brigham, Erin.
    Sustaining the hope for unity : ecumenical dialogue in a postmodern world / Erin Brigham.
        p.   cm.
    "A Michael Glazier book."
    Includes bibliographical references (p.   ) and index.
    ISBN 978-0-8146-8022-3 — ISBN 978-0-8146-8023-0 (e-book)
    1. Ecumenical movement.   2. Christian Union.   3. Church—Unity.   4. Postmodernism—Religious aspects—Christianity.   5. National Council of the Churches of Christ in the United States of America.   I. Title.

BX8.3.B75   2012
262.001'1—dc23   2012001455

Contents

Introduction

In an era shaped by the process of globalization, the concept of "unity" is complex and ambiguous. Globalization, notes Zygmunt Bauman, "divides as much as it unites; it divides as it unites."[1] With the rise of communication technologies and the growing interdependence of the global marketplace, the unity of humanity, in some ways, is more apparent. At the same time, however, globalization has highlighted and intensified all that divides us as a human community. The impact of aggressive free-market capitalism has widened the gap between the rich and the poor across the globe.[2] The homogenizing effects of American culture have been met with resistance from diverse expressions of identity.[3] Considering its ambivalent effects on the quality of human life and the health of the planet, globalization does not inherently make a compelling case for unity. It does, however, invite us to explore the positive and negative consequences of unity and imagine models of unity that are more sustainable and just.

Scholars of religion and theology must respond to the contextual invitation to evaluate approaches to unity. Globalization is one of the "signs of the times" to which contemporary theology must respond, and these theological responses, I argue, must develop critical and creative approaches to community that honor diversity in unity. With respect to the negative effects of globalization, Jonathan Sacks points out that "if

---

[1] Zygmunt Bauman, *Globalization: The Human Consequences* (Cambridge: Polity Press, 1998), 2.

[2] United Nations Development Program Report 1999, in David Held and Anthony McGrew, eds., *The Global Transformations Reader* (Cambridge: Polity Press, 2000), 423–29.

[3] Thomas Friedman, *The Lexus and the Olive Tree: Understanding Globalization* (New York: Anchor Books, 1999), 276–306.

1

religion is not part of a solution, it will certainly be part of the problem."[4] Sacks draws upon the Jewish tradition of covenant to argue for a global community that honors differences. He suggests that a failure to appreciate the "dignity of difference" fuels religious fundamentalism and extreme nationalism and can ultimately lead to destruction on a global scale. These multiple forms of extremism, Sacks argues, emerge in response to perceived threats to identity that accompany globalization. He states:

> We live in the conscious presence of difference. . . . That can be experienced as a profound threat to identity. One of the great transformations from the twentieth to twenty-first centuries is that whereas the former was dominated by the politics of ideology, we are now entering an age of the politics of identity. That is why religion has emerged, after a long eclipse, to become so powerful a presence on the world stage, because religion is one of the great answers to the question of identity. But that, too, is why we face danger. Identity divides.[5]

Assuming Sacks is correct in his assessment of the identity politics that characterize this period of history, it is crucial that religious traditions articulate their identities responsibly. I argue that the responsible assertion of one's religious identity, within the context of globalization, should foster global solidarity. The solidarity that I envision does not eliminate diversity but creates community in such a way that it affirms the "dignity of difference," to use Sacks's language. Solidarity builds just relationships across differences, acknowledging the common human dignity across religious, cultural, and national boundaries. In Pope Benedict XVI's recent social encyclical, *Caritas in Veritate* (CV), he articulates this vision of solidarity for our context: "Globalization is a multifaceted and complex phenomenon which must be grasped in the diversity and unity of all its different dimensions, including the theological dimension. In this way it will be possible to experience and to steer the globalization of humanity in relational terms, in terms of communion and the sharing of goods" (CV 42).[6]

Ecumenism offers a theological reflection on diversity and unity within the context of the Christian religion. The ecumenical movement refers to

---

[4] Jonathan Sacks, *The Dignity of Difference: How to Avoid the Clash of Civilizations* (New York: Continuum, 2002), 9.

[5] Ibid., 10.

[6] Benedict XVI, *Caritas in Veritate*, English translation by the United States Conference of Catholic Bishops (Washington, DC: United States Conference of Catholic Bishops, 2009).

the trajectory of Christian life that promotes Christian unity. Despite the decline of interest in Christian unity that can be observed in the latter half of the twentieth century,[7] I argue that ecumenism is still an important topic of theological reflection. For one thing, ecumenism discerns how to articulate a common Christian identity across traditional divisions. In a globalized context, where identity politics are potentially destructive, religious communities have the responsibility to articulate their identity in nondestructive ways. The global presence of Christianity, like other religious traditions, can be part of the problem or part of the solution to the extremism that Sacks identifies.

In light of the fluidity and hybridity of religious identities, the negotiation of what it means to be Christian together is complicated in a globalized context. Robert Schrieter reminds us that "hybridity is part of life in globalized cultures"[8] and that this reality demands special consideration when speaking to the religious identity of a particular community. Individuals identify with multiple communities, blurring boundaries of categories of belonging. I am convinced, with Schreiter, that the reality of cultural hybridity calls for new ways of negotiating religious identity that celebrates diversity and at the same time facilitates the formation and preservation of community life. Schreiter argues, "One can talk about the construction of the self in postmodernity, but one must also find ways of articulating life in community, since belonging is one of humanity's strongest needs."[9]

The need for belonging and the desire to locate oneself meaningfully in a community has been a strong motivation in my personal and academic life. Growing up in the northwestern United States, I experienced, like many US Americans, a voluntaristic relationship to religion.[10] I resonate with Charles Taylor's description of a secular context as one of multiple options for belief or unbelief. Since "belief in God is no longer axiomatic," faith has become much more privatized and for many individuals, "hard to sustain."[11] Even as a child, I was aware of the multiplicity of choices

---

[7] This is articulated by Walter Kasper, who observes in the ecumenical movement "a spirit of resignation that has often developed over recent years." Kasper, *That They May All Be One: The Call to Unity Today* (New York: Continuum, 2004), 1.

[8] Robert Schreiter, *The New Catholicity: Theology between the Global and Local* (Maryknoll, NY: Orbis, 1997), 76.

[9] Ibid., 78.

[10] Robert Bellah describes this in *Habits of the Heart: Individualism and Commitment in American Life*, 3rd edition (Berkeley: University of California Press, 2007), chap. 9.

[11] Charles Taylor, *A Secular Age* (Cambridge, MA: Harvard University Press, 2007), 3.

surrounding religious identity, and I did not experience myself bound to a particular belief system. I was surrounded by individuals who identified as "spiritual but not religious," a phenomenon that Taylor addresses as a key feature of religious belief today.[12] My Catholic identity had rather shallow roots. It was not integral to my identification with my family, neighborhood, or country. If I would have decided to leave the Catholic Church, I certainly would not have been ostracized or alienated from my family, nor would I have been left without a framework for meaning and moral life. The experience of freedom and ambiguity around religious belonging made me aware of the anxiety to which Sacks refers. I can understand why people retreat from such ambiguity by identifying with religious extremism. I can also understand why individuals retreat from such ambiguity by becoming extremely antireligious. This understanding motivates my reflection on unity, belonging, and the Christian community.

The process of integrating my own religious identity, personal freedom, and sense of belonging has forced me to carefully examine the ways in which multiple narratives have shaped me. My experience as a Roman Catholic, my experience as a woman of European descent, my background in a working-class, rural family from Montana—all of these factors have shaped my identity and my approach to community, making the concept of "belonging" complicated and unstable. My approach to unity, which I articulate in this book, has been shaped by an amalgamation of narratives. Identifying the contextual nature of all approaches to unity is the first step in the development of my thesis.

I realize that I have always responded to the "Why Christian unity?" question based on my own religious experience and theological perspective. This realization has impressed upon me the ways in which diverse self-understandings of Christian communities complicate the task of defining the goal of Christian unity. My approach to ecumenism has been shaped by post–Vatican II Catholic ecclesiology. Theologians are still interpreting the significance of the Second Vatican Council on the ecclesial self-understanding of the Catholic Church.[13] However, in order to articulate my own ecclesiological perspective, I would like to note some key themes of the conciliar documents that have impacted contemporary Catholic ecclesiology. In 1979 Karl Rahner suggested that we should consider "Vatican II as the first major official event in which

---

[12] Ibid., 505–35.

[13] See Ormond Rush, *Still Interpreting Vatican II: Some Hermeneutical Principles* (New York: Paulist Press, 2004), introduction.

the Church actualized itself precisely as a *world Church*."[14] His observation is grounded in the fact that the Second Vatican Council was made up of bishops from all over the world, breaking out of the Eurocentric expression of the church. The principle of episcopal collegiality was lifted up at the council as a physical manifestation of the catholic and communal nature of the church. *Lumen Gentium* (LG), the Second Vatican Council's Dogmatic Constitution on the Church, states, "This same collegiate power can be exercised in union with the pope by the bishops while living in different parts of the world, provided the head of the college summon them to collegiate action, or at least approve or freely admit the corporate action of the unassembled bishops, so that a truly collegiate act may result" (LG 22).[15]

The emphasis on episcopal collegiality provides a framework for understanding the catholicity of the church as a universal communion of local churches. The council describes the individual bishop as "the visible source and foundation of unity in their own particular Churches" (LG 23), while at the same time the bishop exists in a college that is in service of the unity of the universal church. *Lumen Gentium* frames the communion of the local and universal church, stating, "This multiplicity of local Churches, unified in a common effort, shows all the more resplendently the catholicity of the undivided Church" (LG 23). Roger Haight suggests that

> Various levels and meanings of communion run through Vatican II: a new emphasis on the local church allows one to view the whole church as a communion of churches under one head; the idea of a *collegium* of bishops, each with his local responsibility for his own church and, as member of the college, a responsibility for the church at large, supports the notion that the whole church is a communion.[16]

The development of communion ecclesiology opened the door for a greater acknowledgment of the contextual reality of local churches and gave way to a more dynamic understanding of catholicity as an expression

---

[14] Karl Rahner, "Towards a Fundamental Theological Interpretation of Vatican II," in *Theological Studies* 40, no. 4 (December 1979): 717.

[15] All translations of the documents of the Second Vatican Council are taken from Austin Flannery, ed., *Vatican Council II*, vol. 1, *The Conciliar and Post Conciliar Documents*, new rev. ed. (New York: Costello Publishing, 1996).

[16] Roger Haight, *The Christian Community in History*, vol. 2, *Comparative Ecclesiology* (New York: Continuum, 2005), 424.

of diversity in unity. A reemerging question in ecumenical dialogue is how to balance diversity and commonality, the particular and the universal. The Catholic Church, which understands itself to be a "world church," to use Rahner's words, offers a unique contribution to ecumenical conversations about catholicity.

Lifting up the collegial nature of the church also reframed the structure of ecclesial authority, providing a balance to the First Vatican Council's (1870) focus on the central authority of the pope. The Roman Catholic understanding of the role of the pope in maintaining ecclesial unity is still a major obstacle in ecumenical dialogue. John Paul II acknowledged this challenge in his 1995 encyclical, *Ut Unum Sint* (UU), inviting a conversation on how to understand papal centrality in such a way that promotes Christian unity:

> Whatever relates to the unity of all Christian Communities clearly forms part of the concerns of the primacy. As Bishop of Rome I am fully aware, as I have reaffirmed in the present Encyclical Letter, that Christ ardently desires the full and visible communion of all those Communities in which, by virtue of God's faithfulness, his Spirit dwells. I am convinced that I have a particular responsibility in this regard, above all in acknowledging the ecumenical aspirations of the majority of the Christian Communities and in heeding the request made of me to find a way of exercising the primacy which, while in no way renouncing what is essential to its mission, is nonetheless open to a new situation. (UU 95)[17]

In this text John Paul II expresses a number of theological principles that shape Roman Catholic approaches to ecumenism, including the conviction that Christ calls all Christians to be one, that Christ's Spirit dwells in communities that are not in full, visible communion with the Catholic Church, and that the same Spirit compels us toward full, visible unity.

John Paul II's perspective echoes the ecumenical perspective outlined at Vatican II. *Lumen Gentium* declares:

> This is the sole Church of Christ which in the Creed we profess to be one, holy, catholic and apostolic, which our Savior, after his resurrection, entrusted to Peter's pastoral care, commissioning him and the other apostles to extend and rule it, which he raised up for all ages as "the pillar and mainstay of the truth." This Church constituted and

---

[17] John Paul II, *Ut Unum Sint*, English translation by the United States Conference of Catholic Bishops (Washington, DC: United States Conference of Catholic Bishops, 1995).

organized as a society in the present world, subsists in the Catholic Church, which is governed by the successor of Peter and by the bishops in communion with him. Nevertheless, many elements of sanctification and of truth are found outside of its visible confines. Since these are gifts belonging to the Church of Christ, they are forces impelling towards Catholic unity. (LG 8)

The Second Vatican Council's decision to declare that the church of Christ "subsists in" the Catholic Church rather than identifying them conterminously marks an important shift in the Roman Catholic approach to ecumenism. This ecclesiological statement provided the foundation for the Second Vatican Council's Decree on Ecumenism, *Unitatis Redintegratio* (UR). The document expresses the need for ecclesial renewal and personal conversion in the ecumenical movement. In order to get to know other Christians, we have to first adopt a posture of humility and respect. The text states:

There can be no ecumenism worthy of the name without interior conversion. For it is from newness of attitudes of mind, from self-denial and unstinted love, that desires of unity take their rise and develop in a mature way. We should therefore pray to the Holy Spirit for the grace to be genuinely self-denying, humble, gentle in the service of others and to have an attitude of brotherly generosity toward them. (UR 7)

The tone of *Unitatis Redintegratio* follows the council's notably optimistic, humble, and open stance toward the world, other Christians, and people of other faiths. In his historical analysis of the Second Vatican Council, John O'Malley suggests that there was a paradigm shift characterized by a move from a hierarchically ordered, perfect society to a nontriumphalistic understanding of the church as the people of God.[18] Emphasizing the church as the people of God allowed Vatican II to articulate an ecclesiology that located God's activity outside of the church, while also maintaining the belief that the Catholic Church offers the fullest expression of Christ's presence and mission. *Lumen Gentium*'s chapter "The People of God" begins with God's desire for union with all people and describes how God has drawn people into this union throughout history. The text claims that this union is made most visible in the Catholic Church, who labors for the unity of humankind. All people, it states, "are

---

[18] John O'Malley, *Tradition and Transition: Historical Perspectives on Vatican II* (Lima, OH: Academic Renewal Press, 2002), 65.

called to this catholic unity which prefigures and promotes universal peace. And in different ways to it belong, or are related: the Catholic faithful, others who believe in Christ, and finally all mankind, called by God's grace to salvation" (LG 13). Understanding itself as related to humanity through a spectrum of relationships, rather than through a strict separation between the saved and the not-saved, has allowed the Catholic Church to enter more fully into ecumenical dialogue.

After Vatican II the official Catholic approach to ecumenism could not be reduced to the "return to the true church" mentality that dominated preconciliar ecclesiology.[19] One of the reasons for this shift was the self-examination of the Catholic Church and the realization that the church could not be identified with the kingdom of God. This is expressed in the image of the church on a pilgrimage throughout history. The Second Vatican Council's use of the image of the church as pilgrim, I argue in this book, is particularly helpful in ecumenical dialogue as it emphasizes the eschatological quality of church. *Lumen Gentium* states:

> The Church, to which we are all called in Christ Jesus, and in which by the grace of God we acquire holiness, will receive its perfection only in the glory of heaven, when will come the time of the renewal of all things. (LG 48)

> For if we continue to love one another and to join in praising the Most Holy Trinity—all of us who are sons of God and form one family in Christ—we will be faithful to the deepest vocation of the Church and will share in a foretaste of the liturgy of perfect glory. (LG 51)

Acknowledging that the church on earth is a real but imperfect sign of the church in its fullness, Vatican II emphasized the eschatological dimension of the entire Christian church. Acknowledging that we have a partial and imperfect understanding of the church invites us to consider with openness the development of the Church as it grows in holiness. This is an important consideration in ecumenical dialogue because it challenges any exclusive claim to the one Church of Christ. In effect, it creates a space for ecclesiological diversity in the conversation about what the one Church of Christ should look like.

---

[19] This position is exemplified by Pope Pius XI in his Encyclical *Mortalium Animos* (1928) in which he states, "You know well, Venerable Brethren, how We desire their [non-Catholic Christians] return; and We wish all Our children to know it and not only they of the Catholic world but all who are separated from Us." Pius XI, *Mortalium Animos*, trans. Rev. R. McGowan (Washington, DC: National Catholic Welfare Conference, 1928).

In this book, I argue for an eschatological understanding of Christian unity that sustains the churches' commitment to ecumenical dialogue in a context of pluralism and ambiguity. My perspective has been shaped by the ecclesiology of Vatican II and the Catholic Church's postconciliar approach to ecumenism. Coupled with this theological perspective, I draw upon insights of contemporary critical theory, particularly the work of Jürgen Habermas as well as critical expansions of his thought by Seyla Benhabib and Maria Pia Lara. Contemporary critical theory allows me to develop a framework for dialogue that avoids relativism and positivism by acknowledging the contextual nature of all theological truth claims as well as the potential for these claims to speak intelligibly and critically outside of their particular contexts. I argue that contemporary critical theory offers an epistemological framework for dialogue that addresses the current ecumenical climate, which I characterize by the recognition of ecclesiological pluralism, uncertainty about the nature of the goal of the ecumenical movement, and a lack of ecumenical commitment and/ or optimism from many Christians.

The ecumenical movement faces particular challenges and opportunities as it enters into the twenty-first century. Ecumenist Martin Conway suggests that the assessment provided by the first general secretary of the World Council of Churches, Willem A. Visser 't Hooft, can be applied to the ecumenical climate today. In 1968 Visser 't Hooft stated:

> The present ecumenical situation can only be described in the paradoxical statement that the ecumenical movement has entered into a period of reaping an astonishingly rich harvest, but that precisely at this moment, the movement is more seriously called into question than ever before.[20]

The mobility and rapid communication facilitated by the process of globalization has certainly had an impact on Christianity in general and the ecumenical movement in particular. Christians now have the opportunity to encounter each other across regional, cultural and confessional boundaries. The global diversity of Christianity is more apparent than

---

[20] Willem A. Visser 't Hooft, "The Mandate of the Ecumenical Movement," in Norman Goodall, ed., *The Uppsala Report 1968* (Geneva: WCC Publications, 1968), 316. Martin Conway refers to this quote and applies it to the contemporary context in Martin Conway, "Under Public Scrutiny," in John Briggs, Mercy Amba Oduyoye, and Georges Tsetsis, eds., *The History of the Ecumenical Movement*, vol. 3, *1968–2000* (Geneva: WCC Publications, 2004), 433.

ever and has increased the potential for establishing solidarity across differences. Returning to Sacks's insistence upon the ambivalent nature of globalization, I argue that the increased connectivity of Christians across the globe does not necessarily lead to solidarity. We need an approach to unity that speaks to the context of pluralism and ambiguity.

The relevance of the ecumenical movement has been called into question from a variety of locations within and outside of the Christian church. Evangelical Christians have criticized the ecumenical movement for "watering down" biblical mandates and emphasizing the social mission of the church rather than the mission to convert the nonbaptized to Christianity.[21] Likewise, Orthodox Christians have criticized the World Council of Churches for promoting secular ecumenism that engages in social issues instead of prioritizing theological dialogue on faith and doctrine.[22] On the other hand, some Christians view the ecumenical movement as a hindrance to progressive social and theological movements in Christian churches. Some Christians that do not support the ecumenical movement are not coming from a critical perspective. Many Christians, in fact, are apathetic to the ecumenical movement because they are content with confessional diversity. Walter Kasper states:

> The fact that ecumenism is facing a critical moment cannot be denied. There is a widespread conviction that traditional differences are irrelevant for the majority of people today and could be simply overlooked. The "wild ecumenism" that has ensued has led, as a counter-reaction, to the emergence of a new confessionalism. The ecumenical movement has been held responsible for the development of relativism and indifference in questions of faith. . . . Thus, a new atmosphere of mistrust, self-defense and withdrawal has often emerged within confessional compartments.[23]

Following Kasper's description, basing my approach on the aforementioned theological convictions, and assuming that ecumenism is a valuable endeavor, I ask what will sustain ecumenical dialogue in such a context. I do not think that a single approach will create the kind of inclusive participation and commitment to ecumenism that I consider

---

[21] Conway, "Under Public Scrutiny," 440–41.

[22] Orthodox Task Force 1998, "Orthodox-WCC Relations," in Thomas Fitzgerald and Peter Boutenoff, eds., *Turn to God, Rejoice in Hope: Orthodox Reflections on the Way to Harare* (Geneva: WCC, 1998), 175–76.

[23] Kasper, *That They May All Be One*, 1.

to be desirable. I think that multiple approaches, in critical conversation with each other, are needed to address the particular challenges that the ecumenical movement is facing. The approach that I present emerges out of a particular trajectory of Western thought. I consider a developed version of Habermasian critical theory to be especially helpful in this context for the following reasons: it emerges out of a postmodern context and speaks to the pluralism and ambiguity of such a context, it rejects relativism and positivism through the framework of communicative rationality, it articulates a way to achieve social coordination among different perspectives, and it aims for inclusive and dominance-free discourse that I understand to be necessary to create solidarity.

Habermas responds critically and constructively to the postmodern context by developing a framework of communicative rationality. In doing so, he makes a case for the possibility of context-transcending reason that takes into account the particular and historically embedded nature of thought and escapes some of the pitfalls of modernity. The difference between the rationalism of Habermas and the rationalism of Immanuel Kant is significant. While Kant locates reason in the a priori capacities of the thinking individual, Habermas locates reason in the communicative competence of multiple subjects. In other words, Habermas thinks that we exercise rationality through the use of language. Focusing on the level of the speech act itself, Habermas argues that when we say something, we also do something. Specifically, he suggests that we automatically raise a claim to validity that appeals to the rational capacities of the hearer. This framework proposes an understanding of reason that is both particular and universal because the speech act is always embedded in a particular context but also makes a validity claim that transcends that context.

Habermas presents communicative rationality as an alternative to the logocentric model of reason that has dominated Western thought.[24] Joining postmodern thinkers in critiquing this approach to reason, Habermas argues that a postmetaphysical context necessitates an approach to reason that accounts for the historical and contextual nature of thought.[25] Communicative rationality, he argues, provides an alternative to the relativism

---

[24] Following Habermas's description in *Postmetaphysical Thinking*, I am using the concept of logocentrism to refer to the privileging of theory over practice, allowing ideas to be imagined as disembodied and distinct from particular contexts. See Jürgen Habermas, *Postmetaphysical Thinking*, trans. William Hohengarten, (Cambridge, MA: MIT Press, 1992), 6.

[25] Ibid., 39–44.

that occurs in radical deconstructionism and to the positivism that has been inherited in the logocentric model of reason.

Relativism and positivism can both be problematic in the interest of promoting Christian unity. A relativist might avoid dialogue on potentially divisive theological topics because he or she considers all arguments to be equally relevant. Kasper critiques this approach, which assumes that "traditional differences are irrelevant."[26] Positivism can be observed in Christians that consider their tradition to be the only valid expression of Christianity. This attitude can be observed in the emergence of the "new confessionalism" to which Kasper refers.[27] These positions both contradict my understanding of Christian unity as an eschatological reality. The fullness of the Church, not yet realized, should always compel us to grow and must be accompanied by an ongoing process of conversion. Being accountable to the one Church of Christ not yet fully realized pushes us beyond relativism into a challenging process of discernment about the nature of the Church.

Habermas provides an epistemological framework for the kind of dialogue that transcends relativism and positivism in his theory of communicative action. Habermas's theory of communicative action describes how people coordinate social action through communication. Successful communicative action occurs when individuals achieve agreement on criticizable validity claims that are implicitly raised in the communicative encounter. This kind of coordination can only occur when validity claims are freely exchanged and the force of the most rational argument compels the agreement. Social coordination can result from rational or nonrational means. For example, a society can be organized around a dictatorship that uses manipulation or force to maintain social structure. As a critical theorist, Habermas maintains that reason frees a society from ideologies that bind them together and allows people to achieve social coordination through noncoercive means. Habermas distinguishes the social coordination achieved by communicative action from forms of social coordination that are achieved by nonrational means. Habermas describes this type of action as strategic, in which one communicator uses manipulation, bargaining, or coercion to facilitate agreement.

How can we distinguish between communicative action and strategic action in actual contexts? Habermas suggests that we can distinguish

---

[26] Kasper, *That They May All Be One*, 1.
[27] Ibid., 1.

between communicative action and strategic action by the goal of the communicative encounter. Communicative action is always guided by the goal of mutual understanding, which implies an agreement on the validity claims raised. Habermas claims that mutual understanding is the original telos of all language use because it is necessarily prior to the achievement of an additional outcome. When the communicative encounter is shaped by a secondary goal, which may or may not be disclosed to the hearer, the communicators are engaged in strategic action. In other words, Habermas's theory exposes how the goal of an interaction influences the communicators' approach to the interaction. In this framework, rationality provides a means to avoid the imposition of an agenda into communication, freeing participants to truly understand each other.[28]

As a goal-oriented endeavor, ecumenism can benefit from these theoretical insights. The goal of ecumenism, as described by Jeffrey Gros, Eamon McManus, and Ann Riggs, is "to unite in full communion all Christians in the one Church of Christ from their state of division."[29] This formulation of Christian unity is limited, however, in light of the diversity of approaches to ecumenism. For example, free churches such as Quakers and Mennonites that emphasize the invisible nature of the Church challenge the focus on visible expressions of Christian unity. On the other hand, Orthodox churches that understand Christian unity to be maintained in the visible structures of their ecclesial tradition challenge attempts to broaden understandings of Christian unity. Therefore, declaring that the goal of ecumenism is visible unity among Christians is much easier than defining what that goal means. I suggest, following Habermas's theoretical insights, that the way that we define the goal will shape our approach to that goal.

Critics of Habermas are quick to point out that his commitment to reason can lead to some theoretical blind spots. One can identify strengths and weaknesses in his rationalist approach. Overly rationalistic approaches can ignore multiple ways of thinking and communicating, such as artistic and symbolic expressions of thought. The rationalist tradition of Western thought, as postmodern critics point out, has tended to emphasize the universal over the particular and the theoretical over the

---

[28] For Habermas's distinction between strategic and communicative action, see Habermas, "Social Action, Purposive Activity and Communication," in Maeve Cooke, ed., *On the Pragmatics of Communication* (Cambridge, MA: MIT Press, 1998), 119–29.

[29] Jeffrey Gros, Eamon McManus, and Ann Riggs, eds., *Introduction to Ecumenism* (New York: Paulist Press, 1998), 74.

practical. Convinced by the objectives of critical theory, I suggest that the primary strength of rationalism is that it can tap into the emancipatory potential of reason. The trajectory of critical theory out of which Habermas emerges argues that individuals and societies can examine their beliefs and cultural practices reflexively, allowing for critical engagement and transformation. Through the use of critical reason, we are not bound by the biases of our inherited traditions. At its best, the assertion that we can achieve a critical distance from our embedded knowledge opens the door for ideology critique. At its worst, this idea can lead to the myth of objectivity, which ignores the contextual nature of thought. Habermas overcomes many of the problems associated with the modern conception of reason through the framework of communicative rationality. At the same time, Habermas's understanding of reason does not provide adequate consideration for artistic, nonlinguistic, and religious truth claims. Not only does this limitation create specific problems for this project, it also creates a theoretical gap in Habermas's epistemology.

From a Roman Catholic perspective, faith and reason are not opposed but complimentary, needing each other for mutual correction and guidance. The relationship between faith and reason has been a topic of ongoing theological debate that is beyond the scope of this introduction.[30] Suffice it to say that the Catholic theological tradition offers resources to challenge the isolation of reason from religious belief and practice. Drawing upon this perspective, I argue that Habermas's theory of communicative rationality has a place for religious truth claims, but the full potential of his theoretical perspective in this area has not been developed thoroughly. I think that Habermas's critique of a logocentrism lays the foundation to talk about the relationship between faith and reason in a postmodern context. I will explore this potential in chapter 1, pointing out some of the weaknesses in Habermas's theory of religion and proposing a way forward in articulating the place of religious truth claims in Habermas's epistemology.

Feminist theorists have been particularly helpful in addressing some of the weaknesses of Habermas's thought.[31] I will focus on two feminist thinkers who locate themselves in the trajectory of Habermasian critical theory, while departing from his position in significant ways. Seyla Benhabib and Maria Pia Lara draw upon and critique Habermas's

[30] For an introduction to this conversation, see Richard McBrien, *Catholicism*, rev. ed. (New York: HarperCollins, 1994), 14–16.

[31] See Johanna Meehan, ed., *Feminists Read Habermas: Gendering the Subject of Discourse* (London: Routledge, 2005).

critical theory in ways that I think are particularly helpful in discerning the nature of religious truth claims. Benhabib critiques Habermas's
tendency toward universalism in his theory of ethics and morality. As a
critical theorist, Benhabib remains committed to the possibility of conceptualizing universals while opposing "abstract universalism" that does
not account for particularity. She proposes a framework of interactive
universalism that I think is particularly helpful for accounting for the
contextual and universal nature of religious truth claims.[32] Lara takes this
concept further, arguing for the rational status of narrative. She suggests
that narratives bridge the private and public, as they serve to transform
the public identity of a particular group.[33]

I draw upon these feminist insights to develop a framework of religious truth claims and communicative rationality, arguing that religious
claims function as narratives that allow the truth claims of a particular
community to carry critical significance in the public sphere. Religious
truth claims do not fit neatly into Habermas's understanding of rationality. Habermas scholar Maeve Cooke suggests that religious claims
are rational in a particular way and therefore should be distinguished
from other forms of truth claims in Habermas's theory. Cooke suggests
that "religious validity claims destabilize the very distinction between
universal and non-universal validity claims."[34] Accepting this to be the
case based on my understanding of religious validity claims as located
in a particular community but also carrying the potential of public relevance, I argue that Lara's concept of narrative is especially pertinent to
religious truth. As narratives, religious truth claims generate and solidify
a collective identity while also serving to express that identity publicly. In
other words, religious narratives bridge the private experience of believers and the "public" outside of that particular tradition. I do not want to
delineate a sharp contrast between public and private, because I believe
that they mutually shape each other. In this context, I am using the word
"public" to refer to the space where individuals or communities of differing traditions and identities come together to express their own interests.

[32] Seyla Benhabib, *Situating the Self: Gender, Community and Postmodernism in
Contemporary Ethics* (New York: Routledge, 1992).

[33] Maria Pia Lara, *Moral Textures: Feminist Narratives in the Public Sphere* (Berkeley:
University of California Press, 1999).

[34] Maeve Cooke, "Salvaging and Secularizing the Semantic Contents of Religion:
The Limitations of Habermas' Postmetaphysical Proposal," in *The International Journal
of Philosophy and Religion* 60 (2006): 192.

Ecumenical dialogue creates a public space for the exchange of truth claims that emerge out of a particular tradition. Organizations that facilitate ecumenical dialogue, such as the World Council of Churches (WCC), create, in effect, public spaces for the exchange of religious narratives. Conceptualizing these truth claims as narratives allows me to emphasize their contextual nature while maintaining their intelligibility outside of their context of origin. In this way, each tradition can retain its particularity while also moving toward greater Christian unity. Bringing these traditions into conversation with each other allows us to discover our common story and direct its outcome together. In so doing, Christians have the potential for fostering global solidarity and modeling diversity in unity for the globalized world. The theological commitments that I have delineated and the contextual imperative to model solidarity shape my conviction that Christian unity is worth pursuing and inform my approach to this task.

The majority of the sources I use for this project come from the World Council of Churches.While I recognize that the ecumenical movement extends well beyond the WCC, especially considering the fact that my own tradition is not a full member of the council,[35] the historical significance of the WCC provides a unique entry point into the twentieth-century ecumenical movement. Conversations about the nature of unity that have emerged within the context of the WCC have implications beyond the council because of its size and inclusivity. Therefore, I have chosen to focus my constructive proposal on questions that have emerged within the WCC. Namely, I develop a theoretical framework for dialogue that can be used as a guide to promote fairness and inclusivity within the council and beyond its membership. Incorporating a hermeneutics of retrieval, I highlight the significance of "the Toronto statement," a text developed by the Central Committee of the WCC in 1950 to articulate the council's assumptions about the nature of unity and the role of the

---

[35] The Roman Catholic Church is a full member of the Faith and Order Commission and participates closely with the WCC through the Joint Working Group that was established in 1965. There are multiple reasons why the Catholic Church has refrained from membership in the WCC. One of the primary reasons is the size of the Catholic Church, which could be problematic in terms of fair representation. For a discussion of the theological, organizational, and pastoral considerations with regard to the Catholic Church's membership in the WCC, see Thomas Stransky, "Roman Catholic Membership in the World Council of Churches?" *The Ecumenical Review* 20, no. 3 (July 1968): 205–44.

WCC in promoting that unity.[36] Recognizing the ecclesiological diversity of the Christian churches, the Toronto statement declared that the WCC would remain open to discovering the nature of Christian unity and that joining the WCC does not assume a particular ecclesial self-understanding. I argue that these principles are particularly relevant as the WCC discerns its new ethos after adopting a consensus model of deliberation[37] and as it discerns how to create a space for broader participation with nonmember churches and organizations such as the new Global Christian Forum.[38] Ultimately, this book makes a case for the appropriateness of the Toronto statement in the contemporary conversation on the nature and mission of the WCC in the twenty-first century, as it insists upon ecclesiological neutrality and does not presuppose the nature of Christian unity.

I recently participated in a meeting of the World Council of Churches' Continuation Committee on Ecumenism in the 21st Century. I joined theologians and ministers of various churches from all over the world to discuss how to promote Christian unity in our rapidly changing global context. At a gathering in Belem, Brazil, just weeks before the ninth World Social Forum attracted thousands of people to the city, I was struck by the timeliness of our gathering. The World Social Forum developed in response to the negative effects of globalization. The WSF describes itself as "an open meeting place" for various movements and organizations to come together and imagine alternatives to the model of relationships

[36] WCC Central Committee at Toronto, "The Church, the Churches and the World Council of Churches: The Ecclesiological Significance of the World Council of Churches," in Lukas Vischer, ed., A Documentary History of the Faith and Order Movement 1927–1963 (St. Louis, MO: Bethany Press, 1963), 167–77.

[37] The WCC shifted from a parliamentary model of decision to a consensus model in 2005. See Anne Glynn-Mackoul, "Introduction to Consensus," in Metropolitan Gennadios of Sassima, ed., Grace in Abundance: Orthodox Reflections on the Way to Porto Alegre (Geneva: WCC, 2005), 100–106. I will discuss the motivations for this decision and the implications of it in chapter 4.

[38] The Global Christian Forum began developing in 1998, with its first meeting in 2007, as a way for Christians to participate in the ecumenical movement without necessarily participating in the WCC. Its development was motivated in a particular way by the growing presence of Evangelical and Pentecostal churches who do not share the basis of the WCC. For an introduction, see "Progress towards a Global Christian Forum," in WCC Central Committee Report, From Harare to Porto Alegre 1998–2006 (Geneva: WCC, 2005), 26–27. I will discuss the WCC's relationship with the Global Christian Forum and the implications of this relationship for the larger ecumenical movement in chapter 4.

shaped by neoliberal capitalism.[39] It understands itself as a neutral space (nonpartisan, nonconfessional, etc.) for the exchange of different perspectives. As such, it works to promote solidarity in the contemporary globalized context. I cannot help but notice parallels and differences between this forum and the WCC. Both organizations act as a forum for the exchange of diverse perspectives in the interest of facilitating mutual understanding and global solidarity.

In this book, I argue that the World Council of Churches is in a unique position to serve as a similar forum for communication among Christian churches. The WCC facilitates dialogue across confessional, cultural, and national differences. In doing so, it provides a public space for the free exchange of truth claims in the interest of coming to mutual understanding and common action. Through its modeling of unity in diversity, it can promote global solidarity in a world where difference often leads to destruction. In order for the WCC to accomplish this task, I argue that it must acknowledge fully the diversity that exists among the churches. For this reason, the Toronto statement's insistence upon the ecclesial neutrality of the WCC is still relevant today. As long as there is no single understanding of the church among Christians, the WCC needs to remain ecclesiologically open. We can find hope in this openness if we embrace the eschatological nature of the church, acknowledging that the fullness of Christian unity can only be partially known in history.

I presented this thesis at the Belem meeting of the Continuation Committee on Ecumenism in the 21st Century. In response to my proposal, I was challenged by the suggestion that Habermas's Western rationalist approach would not work in a multicultural context like the WCC. One participant issued a critique that the WCC encompasses individuals from contexts where storytelling is one of the main ways that people communicate, and Habermas's rationalist approach does not recognize this form of self-expression. The critique was valid, as it pointed out the limitations of reason and the difficulty in achieving free and inclusive discourse in real contexts. The participant was right to point out the multiple ways of knowing and communicating that are highlighted in an intercultural encounter. Furthermore, the reality of power dynamics that exist in any communicative encounter across cultures, genders, and so forth, complicates the task of facilitating dominance-free discourse. If

---

[39] World Social Forum website, http://www.forumsocialmundial.org.br (accessed December 20, 2009).

individuals do not experience themselves as able to speak, their positions cannot be represented. In an ideal situation, Habermas's principles of discourse seem plausible. However, in actual contexts, where complex histories and hybrid identities shape one's approach to communication, the possibility of a free exchange of ideas becomes difficult to imagine.

Recognizing that Habermas's approach emerges out of a particular trajectory that speaks to my context, I present it as one possibility among others to be considered as we discern the ecumenical movement in the twenty-first century. While Habermas's understanding of reason is multi-dimensional, accounting for many ways of knowing and communicating, it is still limited. For this reason, Lara's insights into the role of narrative truth claims offer a necessary supplement to Habermas's thought. If we consider the rational nature of narrative, in the sense that narratives are publicly intelligible, then the model of communicative rationality is more applicable to real-life contexts. Considering the way in which narratives bridge the particular and universal, I argue that they are the best way to understand religious truth claims. Lifting up the transformative potential of narrative, then, fills in the gaps of Habermas's limited understanding of religious truth claims.

Despite my theoretical appreciation for Habermas's understanding of consensus as a regulatory principle for ongoing discourse, I found myself frustrated with the process of consensus building as I experienced it in the context of the WCC meeting. The process of reaching consensus can be tedious and time consuming. As participants in the meeting made suggestions, the moderator would continually test the consensus level in the room by inviting participants to raise orange or blue cards, indicating whether they felt warm or cold about the proposal on the floor. I cannot count the number of times that I wanted to end the conversation by making a motion to vote on the issue. It confirmed for me the highly pragmatic approach to decision making to which I am accustomed. I found myself uncomfortable with the ambiguity in the consensus model. The goal of a particular conversation was not always clear, as it was constantly in flux by adding other perspectives. I resonated with the words of former general secretary of the WCC Konrad Raiser about consensus: it challenges a particular ethos.[40]

Despite my frustration with the consensus process, I believe that it is a promising approach to ecumenical dialogue. Throughout the course of the

---

[40] Report of the General Secretary Konrad Raiser, in Diane Kessler, ed., *Together on the Way: Official Report of the Eighth Assembly of the WCC* (Geneva: WCC, 1999), 96–97.

meeting, I discovered the way in which the consensus model broadened participation and created the potential for all voices to be heard. In fact, I noticed that the process itself encouraged storytelling among the participants. Without the pressure of deciding yes or no on a particular issue, participants are invited to give context to their perspectives. If people trust that they will be heard, I think that they are more willing to tell their stories and, in doing so, to make a truth claim about their identities. This is essential in ecumenical dialogue, I argue, because ecumenism should be an ongoing process of discovering how different expressions of the Christian tradition can come together to manifest the unity of the one Church of Christ.

Realizing the possibility of consensus in the context of ecumenical dialogue has implications for contemporary critical theory as well. I argue that the adoption of consensus procedures in the WCC shifts the way that participants engage in the conversations and relate to one another. One of the implications that I would like to stress is the possibility of creating an atmosphere for storytelling as a means for the exchange of truth claims. Observing the application of Habermas's thought in actual contexts highlights the potential of his discourse theory to facilitate dominance-free agreement. Exploring the implications of Habermasian critical theory in the context of ecumenical dialogue, I argue, reveals the rational nature of religious truth claims in that they can enter into a public space intelligibly and critically. This evidence provides a compelling critique of Habermas's limited view on religion. Instead of having to translate religious truth claims into secular language to consider them publicly accessible, we are invited to consider the rational nature of the particular, contextual narratives themselves.

OUTLINE

I develop my approach to ecumenical dialogue in four parts. In chapter 1, I read Habermas's thought with the interest of applying his theoretical perspective to account for religious truth claims. Convinced that Habermas's theory of communicative action provides a unique take on how particular perspectives can achieve mutual understanding, I retrieve his epistemological insights on communicative rationality and bring them into conversation with feminist critiques. In doing so, I present a nuanced version of Habermasian critical theory that takes into account the unique nature of religious truth claims as narrative bridges between the contextual and the universal but at the same time retains his framework of communicative rationality.

I make a case for the applicability of a revised and expanded Habermasian critical approach to ecumenical dialogue in chapter 2 by applying his insights to two historical case studies. Analyzing Zeno's *Henoticon* in the aftermath of the Council of Chalcedon and then analyzing events surrounding the Council of Florence using Habermas's theory of communicative action allows me to highlight why these attempts to facilitate Christian unity ultimately failed. In doing so, I am able to pull out guiding principles for effective ecumenical dialogue today. Namely, dialogue must be grounded in the honest exchange of particular truth claims, and the exchange must be inclusive and dominance-free.

In chapters 3 and 4, I apply these principles gleaned from critical theory to contemporary debates within the World Council of Churches. Using sources that have emerged out of the history of the WCC, I examine questions about the nature of Christian unity and the role of the WCC in facilitating that unity. Specifically, I highlight debates around the appropriateness of the Toronto statement's insistence upon neutrality on the nature of Christian unity. Some ecumenists argue that we should have a more definitive pronouncement on the nature of unity, while others have maintained that neutrality is necessary due to ecclesiological pluralism. These debates, which pertain to the nature of the goal of ecumenical dialogue, invite a consideration of how the goal of a conversation frames the approach to that goal. Using Habermas's distinction between communicative and strategic action, I argue that the goal of ecumenical dialogue needs to be determined discursively. Considering the diversity of ecclesiological perspectives in the conversation on Christian unity, I argue for openness on the question of what unity means.

I propose that the nature of Christian unity and the role of the World Council of Churches in facilitating that unity must be informed by ongoing dialogue; therefore, it cannot be presupposed definitely. Such dialogue can only be sustained through inclusive and dominance-free discourse. Following Habermas, I argue that consensus is always provisional, subject to critique and revision. If discourse is to be truly inclusive and consensus truly noncoercive, the possibility of new insight is always present. This framework locates unity in the process of dialogue rather than in the final goal. Conceived in this way, unity is experienced in the process of consensus formation and is always in flux. Unity is not a neat goal that we can envision and create. Theologically, this invites us to retrieve the eschatological dimension of Christian unity, which *Lumen Gentium* emphasizes in describing the church as a pilgrim community.

1

Communicating Religious Narratives

Habermas has drawn upon and contributed to multiple fields, including philosophy, critical theory, ethics, and political theory. While he does not explicitly address ecumenical dialogue, his developing perspective on religion offers valuable insights on the possibility of bringing into conversation religious truth claims from different contexts, with the potential for agreement. Habermas's theory of communicative action essentially addresses how individuals arrive at context-transcending agreement without disregarding the contextual nature of thought. This chapter presents an overview of Habermas's thought as it relates specifically to the theological conversation around the nature and mission of ecumenical dialogue. More precisely, it explores how diverse perspectives can come to agreement on a "shared truth"[1] without coercion or compromise in an ecumenical context. Although this chapter will not permit an exhaustive treatment of the theory, the major components of Habermas's thought can be organized around the question of how his theory of communicative action provides a way to freely arrive at perspective-transcending truth in a pluralistic context.

This theory of communicative action addresses both explicitly and implicitly the nature of religious truth claims and the possibility of reaching meaningful consensus across the boundaries of particular faith communities. Discovering the rational potential of religious truth claims, I argue, is essential for identifying the possibility of religious truth claims to speak intelligibly outside of their context of origin. Ecumenical dialogue necessitates this public articulation of particular religious truth claims because,

---

[1] In this context, I am using the language of shared truth to refer to agreement on validity claims that emerge in a discursive encounter. I am following Habermas's assumption that we can adopt a reflexive stance toward our context and come to an agreement with someone from a different context. I do not mean to suggest that we can escape our context and arrive at a disembodied truth, but I want to emphasize the possibility of reaching consensus across diverse perspectives.

though Christians are professing the same faith, the diverse expressions of this faith require communication across contextual differences. Again, my understanding of the church comes out of my Roman Catholic context. Therefore, when I enter into ecumenical dialogue with a Lutheran on the topic of ecclesiology, I can expect considerable overlap in our faith, but I must also find a way to communicate cross-contextually. This chapter will explore the development and implications of Habermas's theory of communicative action with particular attention to his understanding of religion and religious truth claims in order to lay the foundation for a critical approach to ecumenical dialogue that I will develop in subsequent chapters. Habermas's perspective on religion has shifted throughout the maturation of his thought. He has moved away from an early dismissal of religion as a premodern and prerational medium for social cohesion toward an appreciation of the significant role that Christianity has played in shaping the Western rational tradition.[2]

Habermas has just recently begun to offer a sympathetic analysis of the role of religion in modern societies. His recent writings have reflected his interest in the relationship between religion and the modern state as he explores the nature of religious and secular discourse.[3] As such, Habermas has yet to fully integrate his understanding of religion into his theory of modernity, rationality, and discourse, leaving readers to wonder how religious discourse fits into his framework of communicative rationality. This chapter will begin to systematize his perspective on religious truth claims and the role of religion in modern society as I address the question of how to arrive at unity in plurality using Habermas's theory of communicative action.

This chapter will address four topics that connect Habermas's thought to ecumenical dialogue. First, I present Habermas's critical analysis of modernity and postmodernity in his development of a postmetaphysical perspective. This is helpful for understanding the contemporary context of ecumenism, which is marked by pluralism and ambiguity. Following this, I present Habermas's framework of communicative rationality and discuss the significance of this framework in the development of his theory of communicative action. Habermas develops an account of

---

[2] Jürgen Habermas and Joseph Ratzinger, *The Dialectics of Secularization: On Reason and Religion*, trans. B. McNeil (San Francisco: Ignatius Press, 2006), 44.

[3] Jürgen Habermas, "Religion in the Public Sphere: Cognitive Presuppositions for the 'Public Use of Reason' by Religion and Secular Citizens," in *Between Naturalism and Religion*, trans. Ciaran Cronin (Malden, MA: Polity Press, 2008), 114–47.

communicative rationality in response to this postmetaphysical context, offering it as way to avoid positivism and relativism. This serves as the epistemological foundation for my analysis of ecumenical dialogue. Next, I analyze Habermas's discourse theory and his development of a multidimensional theory of truth. In this section, I draw upon other critical theorists to explore how religious truth claims challenge some of Habermas's assumptions about rationality. Finally, I lay out Habermas's theory of modern society, addressing how Habermas understands social cohesion and why he makes a case for critical theory. This conversation invites us to consider the role of religion in the public sphere and will also inform my understanding of the WCC as a forum for ecumenical dialogue. I suggest that Habermas's insistence upon the public voice of religion[4] has significant implications for his understanding of the nature of religious truth claims and has yet to be systematized into his thought. The integration of religious truth claims into Habermas's thought, I suggest, provides a compelling approach to ecumenical dialogue that presents religious truth claims as bridges between the particular and the universal. This framework accounts for the particularity of each Christian tradition while also making a case for unity across diverse contexts.

POSTMETAPHYSICAL THOUGHT
AND THE POSSIBILITY OF RELIGION

Habermas has been described as "the last great rationalist."[5] In order to understand Habermas, however, we have to ask what kind of rationalist he is. Habermas argues that "the unity of reason only remains perceptible in the plurality of its voices."[6] This statement reveals two important theoretical commitments that characterize Habermas's thought. First, he is interested in retrieving the Enlightenment category of reason and

---

[4] Habermas argues that religion has an irreplaceable role in modern societies, as it addresses ethical-existential questions that philosophy cannot, as yet, adequately answer. He is interested in how religious voices can contribute to the development of norms and policy, but he argues that religious language must be translated into publicly accessible language on the level of formal policy. See Jürgen Habermas, "Religion in the Public Sphere," in *Between Naturalism and Religion*, 114–47.

[5] Thomas McCarthy, introduction to Jürgen Habermas, *The Theory of Communicative Action*, vol. 1, *Reason and the Rationalization of Society*, trans. Thomas McCarthy (Boston: Beacon Press, 1981), vi.

[6] Jürgen Habermas, *Postmetaphysical Thinking*, trans. William Hohengarten, (Cambridge, MA: MIT Press, 1992), 117.

critically appropriating it in a postmodern context. Second, he recognizes the reality of pluralism that has debunked the Enlightenment bias toward universals. These two commitments are indicative of his approach to modernity and his understanding of postmetaphysical thinking.

As the current of twentieth-century philosophy moved away from rationality through the various postmodern critiques of the Enlightenment, Habermas has maintained a theoretical commitment to reason. His understanding of reason, however, does not fit into the Enlightenment paradigm that many postmodern thinkers reject.[7] Reason, for Habermas, is not exercised by a solitary subject grasping objective truths. Rather, Habermas conceives a model of communicative reason that seeks to establish context-transcending universals without relying on timeless axioms.[8]

Habermas argues that the Enlightenment model of reason lacks credibility in a postmetaphysical context, which he characterizes by four shifts in Western thought: (1) the recognition of scientific rationality that challenges the privileged role of philosophy, (2) the challenge to the classical privileging of theory over practice, (3) the rise of historical consciousness, and (4) the shift away from the philosophical paradigm of consciousness to the paradigm of language.[9] Habermas develops his major ideas in response to these four features of postmetaphysical thinking. These features are worth exploring here because they offer a framework for understanding how Habermas locates religion in a postmetaphysical context.

---

[7] See Habermas's *Philosophical Discourses of Modernity* in which he critiques Foucault, Derrida, and other postmodern thinkers who can be characterized by their critiques of the Enlightenment model of reason. Habermas argues that deconstructionism does not offer a viable alternative to the subject-centered model of reason. He suggests that communicative rationality offers the best alternative in that it avoids relativism and positivism. Jürgen Habermas, "An Alternative Way out of the Philosophy of the Subject: Communicative versus Subject-Centered Reason," in *The Philosophical Discourses of Modernity*, trans. Frederick Lawrence (Cambridge, MA: MIT Press, 1987), 294–326.

[8] I do not mean to suggest that Habermas resolves the debate on how to establish universals in a postmetaphysical context. I think that his theory is incomplete without integrating feminist critiques of his universalist assumptions, which I explore later in the chapter. At this point, I am laying out a foundation of Habermas's theory to set up a constructive engagement with his thought.

[9] Habermas, *Postmetaphysical Thinking*, 33–34.

Traditional philosophical metaphysics, which describes the "universal, immutable and necessary,"[10] are no longer possible after the Kantian critique of pure reason. Kant demonstrated that the way we conceive of ideas is shaped by our prior categories of thought. In other words, he pointed out that we always think from somewhere. In doing so, Kant pointed out the cognitive limits of our capacity to use reason and ushered in a new role for modern philosophy. Postmetaphysical philosophy lacks the credibility to describe the totality of existence because its authority to name universal truths has been questioned. Therefore, in the modern post-Kantian context, philosophy can be understood as a mediator between the taken-for-granted knowledge that shapes our daily lives and the specialized knowledge of the natural and cultural sciences. Philosophy (and theology, Habermas adds) still has an important function in this context; however, it must exercise this function in conversation with other forms of knowledge.

Habermas retains many features of Kantian thought, including the insistence on the emancipatory role of reason. For Habermas and other critical theorists, the ability to use reason allows us to transcend to some extent the contextual limits of our thinking. This is not to say that we can step outside of our inherited linguistic/conceptual framework, which, as Kant illustrated, shapes our very categories of thought. However, it does mean that we can reflexively question our taken-for-granted knowledge. Habermas's understanding of reason as emancipatory emerges out of his critical appropriation of Karl Marx within the framework of the Frankfurt School of critical theory. Marx laid the foundations for critical theory by demonstrating that knowledge is never disinterested but always serves the desires and goals of a particular individual or group. When such interests are concealed, knowledge becomes ideology and functions as an instrument of power. The coupling of knowledge and interests, therefore, can serve as a means for the dominant members of a society to manipulate others.

In his development of critical theory, Habermas offers a critical but sympathetic response to Marx's historical materialism. He applauds Marx for reframing the classical relationship between theory and practice, which had privileged theoretical knowledge over its practical implications. Habermas argues that in Marx's analysis of human interaction in the negotiation of labor, he successfully demonstrates the practical

---

[10] Ibid., 13.

intention behind taken-for-granted knowledge.[11] The dynamic of development, from Habermas's perspective, is distinct from the actual forms that it takes in real historical contexts. Marx fails to acknowledge this distinction, relying on a "history of species" notion of social evolution.[12] This is problematic, according to Habermas, because the conflation of the dynamics of development with particular forms of production does not take into account cross-cultural differences. Our awareness of the historical embeddedness of ideas reveals how they take on different forms according to particular contexts. Habermas stresses this as a primary feature of postmetaphysical thinking. One should note that, even in his earlier work, Habermas resisted philosophical currents that proposed universal categories at the expense of recognizing contextual differences.[13] This awareness is essential for accounting for the contextual nature of religious discourse.

Habermas articulates the framework of communicative rationality against what he identifies as the paradigm of consciousness. Understood within this heavily Cartesian paradigm, rationality is located in the knowing subject's ability to grasp objective truth. This presents an ahistorical and disembodied concept of reason that is no longer viable in a postmetaphysical framework. Within the linguistic turn of post-Hegelian philosophy, Habermas sees the potential for developing an alternative to this problematic understanding of reason. Unfortunately, according to Habermas, all of the postmodern efforts to dismantle subject-centered reason have failed to break out of the paradigm of consciousness and offer an appropriate alternative epistemology.[14] The alternative, Habermas insists, locates reason within the paradigm of language. Habermas develops his framework of communicative rationality from this stance, which allows him to maintain a commitment to reason within a postmetaphysical context.

---

[11] Jürgen Habermas, *Theory and Practice*, trans. John Viertel (Boston: Beacon Press, 1973), 195–252.

[12] Ibid., 195–252.

[13] See Jürgen Habermas, *Communication and the Evolution of Society*, trans. Thomas McCarthy (Boston: Beacon Press, 1979).

[14] Habermas suggests that Hegel was the first thinker to problematize the epistemological assumptions of the Enlightenment. Habermas identifies post-Hegelian thinkers who have since issued critiques of the modern conception of reason. Habermas recognizes the diversity of postmodern perspectives but argues that they all fail to break out of the modernist paradigm of consciousness. See Habermas, *Philosophical Discourses of Modernity*.

For the purposes of this chapter, it is imperative that we ask how Habermas locates religion within the context he describes as postmetaphysical. As I previously mentioned, Habermas's earlier view of religion was precipitously dismissive, so his earlier work does not engage the question of the role of religion within a postmetaphysical context. It is interesting to note, however, the Frankfurt School's rather involved treatment of religion, which Habermas did not carry into his early work despite the fact that the Frankfurt School, particularly its founders Max Horkheimer and Theodor Adorno, provided the foundation for Habermas's development of critical theory. Both of these thinkers were fascinated with the role of religion in society and saw it as an integral part of their interdisciplinary project at the Frankfurt School. Religion, they point out, serves an undeniable function at different levels of society. The transformation of society necessarily involves a transformation of religion, which must come from a self-reflexive critique. Referring specifically to the early Frankfurt School, Eduardo Mendieta suggests that

> in critical theory we find not just a deliberate attempt to think religion *with* religion and *against* religion, but also the urge to rescue theology for the sake of reason. . . . In contrast with the traditional idea that theology is faith-seeking understanding, for the thinkers of the Frankfurt School theology is reason in search of itself by way of the demystification of social reality.[15]

Without going into the details of Horkheimer and Adorno's respective positions on religion, I want to point out that these early critical theorists saw the potential of self-critical religion to have a critical function in society. Thus, they recognized the ability to exercise rationality in the critique of religion and the possibility of religion to articulate rational social criticism. These thinkers shared Habermas's theoretical commitments to postmetaphysical thought: demystifying the role of philosophy as the interpreter of the entirety of existence, recognizing how praxis informs theory, understanding the historical embeddedness of ideas, and appreciating how the linguistic turn transforms the category of reason. However, they were interested in bringing religion into their interdisciplinary intellectual project, recognizing that it could serve the functions of critical theory in the transformation of society. Habermas's recent concern for the role of religion in the public sphere reflects some

---

[15] Eduardo Mendieta, ed., *The Frankfurt School on Religion: Key Writings by the Major Thinkers* (New York: Routledge, 2005), 9–10, emphases in original.

features of the early Frankfurt School, as he considers religious discourse to have a critical function in developing social norms.[16] His earlier understanding of religion, as presented in his *Theory of Communicative Action*, follows the position of Max Weber. As we shall see in the next section, this position leads to a disregard for the potential of religion to exercise a rational, critical function in society.

COMMUNICATIVE RATIONALITY, COMMUNICATIVE ACTION, AND RELIGION

Habermas's early view on religion and society developed alongside his theory of communicative action. His theory of communicative action emerged as a response to Max Weber's understanding of modernization as a process of rationalization.[17] Weber argues that societies become rational when they become more efficient through the differentiation of knowledge into specialized systems, that is, economic and political systems. In premodern societies, social cohesion was maintained through a shared worldview expressed in religious terms. Medieval Christendom exemplified this social reality. Modernization occurs as a disenchantment of these worldviews, according to Weber, and is accompanied by a loss of meaning and the experience of alienation. Through modernization, Weber argues, taken-for-granted knowledge is questioned and worldviews become relativized. The resulting loss of shared meaning poses a threat to social cohesion. Consequently, social cohesion must take on a different form in modern societies. Instead of deferring to the authority of a shared religious worldview, people are bound together in so far as they buy into the legitimacy of social systems.[18]

Habermas agrees with the idea of modernization occurring as a process of rationalization, but he argues that Weber's understanding of rationalization is one-sided since it only accounts for an increase in technical reason that can be observed on the level of social systems. Habermas suggests that modern societies are composed of both systems and lifeworlds. This distinction becomes evident when we consider how we can observe

---

[16] Jürgen Habermas, "Religion in the Public Sphere," in *Between Naturalism and Religion*, 114–47.

[17] Following Habermas's reading of Weber, this refers to Weber's understanding of modernization as a process of rationalization. Jürgen Habermas, *The Theory of Communicative Action*, vol. 1, 143.

[18] Ibid., 186–215.

society from either an internalist or an externalist perspective.[19] The internalist perspective is experienced by a participant in society, who relies on taken-for-granted background knowledge to maintain basic social cohesion in daily life. This is how knowledge functions in the lifeworld. On the other hand, the externalist perspective can be taken when one observes society as a series of social systems—above all, economic and political systems that also function to maintain social cohesion but rely on a process of rational legitimation instead of commonsense knowledge.[20] Habermas does not want to separate these perspectives. He argues that it is impossible to step outside of the lifeworld, but he also maintains that a rationalized society can be characterized by the ability of individuals to adopt a reflexive attitude.[21]

Our ability to adopt a reflexive attitude is dependent upon the shift from a totalizing worldview to a more complex framework of truth. Habermas describes this process through the differentiation of subjective, social, and objective "worlds" or legitimation spheres. In other words, the breakdown of traditional worldviews, as exemplified in medieval Christendom, allows us to make a distinction among subjective, social, and objective knowledge. One can recognize, in a modern society, the difference between empirical truths and social conventions. The distinction of these worlds reflects differentiations in the use of communicative action to maintain social cohesion. Habermas develops the theory of communicative action to describe how we use language to coordinate our social reality. Offering a pragmatic analysis of language, Habermas suggests that every time we use language, we simultaneously make a claim that our speech is objectively true, subjectively sincere, and socially right. The articulation of these types of truth is based upon the typology of three validity spheres or worlds that become differentiated through rationalization. Specifically, when we make a validity claim about what is true, we appeal to the objective world to legitimate our reasons behind the claim. Likewise, we appeal to the social world to legitimate reasons behind a claim to rightness, and we appeal to the subjective world to legitimate our claims to sincerity or truthfulness. This typology reveals

---

[19] Jürgen Habermas, "Actions, Speech Acts, Linguistically Mediated Interactions and the Lifeworld," in Maeve Cooke, ed., *On the Pragmatics of Communication* (Cambridge, MA: MIT Press, 1998), 246–55.

[20] Ibid., 246–55

[21] Habermas, "Some Further Clarifications on the Concept of Communicative Rationality," in Cooke, ed., *On the Pragmatics of Communication*, 310.

the multidimensionality of Habermas's understanding of communicative rationality, which differs significantly from Weber's framework based on instrumental reason alone.[22]

Again, Habermas understands modernization to correspond to an increased efficacy of communicative action, allowing it to replace nonrational forms of social cohesion. Efficacious communicative action occurs when social coordination is achieved through communicative rationality rather than prereflective acceptance of a shared worldview.[23] Rationality serves as the binding force of social interaction when communicative actors are able to freely exchange truth claims that are raised in every speech act. This implies that communicators are able to freely respond yes or no to the validity claims presented implicitly in each use of language. A hearer can respond freely only if he or she understands the claim being raised and the conditions for its acceptance. If there is an undisclosed goal within the communicative encounter, the hearer can be manipulated into agreement. This falls into the category of strategic action, a term Habermas assigns to the type of action that is motivated by personal success and achieved through manipulation or bargaining rather than agreement on validity claims. He differentiates this strategic type of interaction from communicative action as a foundational premise of his theory.[24]

The distinction between communicative and strategic action is a foundational assumption in Habermas's theory. He argues for the primacy of communicative action by developing a formal pragmatic analysis of language. In other words, Habermas seeks to uncover the universal, rational structure behind language use in order to argue that the communicative function of language is the most basic and is prior to any strategic use of language. He approaches this by using the speech-act theory developed by John Austin and John Searle. Austin distinguishes between three aspects of communication: locutionary (saying something), perlocutionary (having an effect on the hearer through saying something), and illocutionary (doing something by saying something).[25] Habermas is particularly interested in the illocutionary aspect of communication, namely, what we do by saying something. In other words, Habermas focuses on the

---

[22] Ibid., 310–17.

[23] Habermas, "Actions, Speech Acts, Linguistically Mediated Interactions and the Lifeworld," in Cooke, ed., *On the Pragmatics of Communication*, 246–55.

[24] Habermas, "Some Further Clarifications of the Concept of Communicative Rationality," in Cooke, ed., *On the Pragmatics of Communication*, 325–33.

[25] Habermas, *Theory of Communicative Action*, vol. 1, 286–95.

action that accompanies our use of language. This emphasis shapes his formal pragmatic analysis of language, upon which he builds his theory of communicative action.

Drawing upon the distinction between perlocutionary and illocutionary acts, Habermas argues that language acts oriented toward reaching understanding are the "original mode" of language.[26] He supports this argument by pointing out that perlocutions are dependent on illocutions and not vice versa. In an illocutionary act, the aims of the speaker are evident. The communicative intent is built into the act itself; it is embedded in the way we use language. Conversely, in the case of perlocutions, the meaning of the speech act is embedded in the intention of the speaker, which may or may not be clear. The perlocutionary aims of the speaker depend on the illocutionary success of the speech act itself. The hearer must understand the speech act in order for any secondary goal to be reached.[27] This makes sense in real-life contexts. For example, if I want my student to read aloud from a textbook, the student must understand what I am saying (illocutionary success) prior to deciding whether to accept the requested outcome (perlocutionary aim).

Habermas describes communicative action as "the type of interaction in which *all* participants harmonize their individual plans of action with one another and thus pursue their illocutionary aims *without reservation*."[28] There cannot be a hidden goal or an asymmetrical relationship between participants in communicative action because the binding force of communicative action must be the intersubjective recognition of the validity claims themselves.[29] Only speech acts that allow speakers to connect criticizable validity claims can be described as communicative action. These validity claims, according to Habermas, are built into the original mode of language itself, facilitating the aim of mutual understanding. Upon this premise, Habermas argues that there is a rational illocutionary binding force that is built into the speech act aimed at mutual understanding in an inherent structure of validity claims. This is how he demonstrates that communicative rationality can be the agent of social integration in a modern society.

Habermas argues that communicative action serves to facilitate social integration differently in premodern and modern societies. This distinction is crucial to Habermas's critique of Weber's concept of modernization

---

[26] Ibid., 288.
[27] Ibid., 289.
[28] Ibid., 294.
[29] Ibid., 305.

as rationalization and helps us understand his early perspective on religion. Habermas suggests that premodern societies relied exclusively on social integration rooted in the lifeworld, albeit one in which consensus rested mainly on totalizing worldviews that were protected by authority structures against communicative challenge. He draws upon Emile Durkheim's theory of social solidarity to suggest how this changes through the process of modernization. In the second volume of *The Theory of Communicative Action*, Habermas refers to Durkheim's concept of the linguistification of the sacred to describe modernization as a learning process. Durkheim posits that social solidarity was traditionally created through the authority of the sacred, which was reinforced through shared symbols and ritual practice. The process of modernization was accompanied by a breakdown of this solidarity as the collective consciousness of the sacred was fragmented. No longer able to rely on a shared worldview, modern societies rely on law that is legitimated through social agreement to maintain solidarity. Habermas builds upon Durkheim's theory to argue that modern social solidarity is achieved through the development of communicative competence, which allows communicative action to replace the authority of the sacred.[30]

When communicative action replaces the role of a totalizing worldview as the primary means of social cohesion, there is an increased demand for efficacious communicative action. When such demands are placed on communicative action, Habermas argues that modern societies must create "relief mechanisms" to assist in maintaining integration. Relief mechanisms emerge in the form of language-independent steering media, namely, money and power. These steering media create social systems that stabilize a rational society without having to rely on the immediacy of rational discourse. When this happens, social systems, rather than the shared lifeworld, function to hold the society together. Habermas describes this type of social coordination as functional integration, distinguishing it from social integration. Social integration is facilitated by communicative action and is grounded in the immediate background knowledge of the lifeworld. Since it is the immediate effect of action aimed at mutual understanding, rationality serves as the binding force of social integration. Functional integration, on the other hand, is facilitated by social systems that give greater range for coordination based on

---

[30] Jürgen Habermas, *The Theory of Communicative Action*, vol. 2, *Lifeworld and System: A Critique of Functionalist Reason*, trans. Thomas McCarthy (Boston: Beacon Press, 1987), 77–110.

strategic action; consequently, functional integration loses the immediate connection to communicative action.[31]

This situation presents the conditions for what Habermas describes as the "colonization of the lifeworld."[32] When strategic action becomes institutionalized in the systems of money and power, the goals of that action can define the identities of members of that society. In other words, when markets and bureaucratic institutions become too pervasive in a society, they change the way that individuals interact and understand themselves in the everyday activity of the lifeworld. Meaning, values, and goals are no longer defined by the taken-for-granted horizon of the lifeworld but by the technical aims of systems. The colonization of the lifeworld leads to the loss of shared meaning and creates problems related to the legitimation of social norms.[33]

While Habermas identifies the problematic process of modern social systems (economic, political, etc.) colonizing the society's lifeworld, he does not want to imply that systems are inherently negative. When systems are informed by the communicative action of the lifeworld, they can provide legitimate social cohesion within a complex and pluralistic context. For example, in an ideal democracy, the political system is shaped by the lifeworld interests of its citizens. Unlike many of his predecessors in critical theory,[34] Habermas does not hold an entirely pessimistic position on rationalization and modernity. Again, Habermas wants to retrieve the theoretical benefits of rationality and appropriate them to the postmetaphysical context. Modern societies, Habermas claims, can use the insights of communicative rationality to resist the colonization of the lifeworld.

This basic structure of Habermas's theory of communicative action allows us to understand his early perspective on religion and to map out the subsequent developments in his perspective. In the first volume of *The Theory of Communicative Action*, Habermas locates his perspective in conversation with Weber, broadening Weber's notion of rationality but agreeing with the concept of the disenchantment of religious worldviews

---

[31] Habermas, "Actions, Speech Acts, Linguistically Mediated Interactions, and Lifeworld," in Cooke, ed., *On the Pragmatics of Communication*, 246–55.

[32] Habermas, *Theory of Communicative Action*, vol. 2, 318–31.

[33] Ibid., 318–31.

[34] Specifically, Horkheimer and Adorno, early theorists of the Frankfurt School, through their interpretation of Weber's rationalization thesis had arrived at the conclusion that a truly emancipated rational society in modernity was impossible. See David Held, *Introduction to Critical Theory: Horkheimer to Habermas* (Berkeley: University of California Press, 1980), 44–70.

in the process of modernization. In the second volume of *The Theory of Communicative Action*, Habermas continues his theory of modernization as a process of disenchantment, this time using Durkheim to couple the linguistification of the sacred and the rationalization of a society.

Considering Habermas's framework of rationalization as the replacement of metaphysical worldviews with communicative action, religion can be understood as obsolete or even detrimental within modern societies. Without a doubt, the role of religion changed in the context of Western modernity. However, scholars of religion and theology have pointed out the limitations of Habermas's early view of religion, which relies too heavily on Weber's secularization thesis.[35] Recent scholarship has debunked Weber's secularization thesis, pointing out that religion still plays an important role in modern societies. In fact, one can observe a resurgence of religious fervor in some contexts, particularly in the global South.[36]

Habermas has responded to these critiques, revising his earlier view on religion and now giving more recognition to the indispensible role of religion in the lifeworld and acknowledging the possibility of religion in the public sphere. As he has engaged in conversations with theologians and religious studies scholars, he has maintained his commitment to postmetaphysical thinking while also acknowledging the ways in which theology has responded to the postmetaphysical shift of modernity. Recognizing that religion remains influential within a modern context, Habermas has rescinded to some extent his evaluation of Weber in *The Theory of Communicative Action*. In 1992 he stated:

> I would also admit that I subsumed rather too hastily the development of religion in modernity with Max Weber under the "privatization of the powers of faith" and suggested too quickly an affirmative answer to the question as to "whether then from religious truths, after the religious world views have collapsed, nothing more and nothing other

---

[35] See Maeve Cooke, "Salvaging and Secularizing the Semantic Contents of Religion: The Limitations of Habermas' Postmetaphysical Proposal," *The International Journal of Philosophy and Religion* 60 (2006): 187–207; and Matthew Mathews, "The Persistence of Religious Meaning in the Critical Theory of Jürgen Habermas," *Soundings* 82 (1999): 383–99.

[36] For a detailed critique of theories of secularization, see Charles Taylor, *A Secular Age* (Cambridge, MA: Harvard University Press, 2007). By illustrating different expressions of secularity, Taylor offers a compelling argument against Weber's understanding of secularization as a decline of religious influence in modern societies. Taylor is most interested in the type of secularism that allows believers and unbelievers to reasonably maintain their worldviews alongside each other.

than the secular principles of a universalist ethics of responsibility can be salvaged, and this means: can be accepted for good reasons, on the basis of insight." This question has to *remain open* from the view of the social scientist. . . . It must also remain open from the viewpoint of the philosopher.[37]

Habermas describes his stance as one of methodological atheism in that he believes that religious language must be translated in order to enter into public discourse with philosophy and social science. At the same time, he advocates for an agnostic openness to the possibility of religion offering something new, unique, or important to public discourse. This allows Habermas to maintain his secular and postmetaphysical commitments without being antireligious.[38]

Habermas even goes beyond openness to postulating that religious truth claims still have an indispensible role in the lifeworld. Religion not only creates solidarity within a community and motivates people toward ethical commitments. Religious beliefs also offer consolation against existential doubts, particularly ones that emerge out of suffering. Philosophy, as yet, cannot provide the same kind of comfort that people seek in religious belief. As early as 1988, Habermas explicitly acknowledged the importance of religion:

> Viewed from without, religion, which has largely been deprived of its worldview functions, is still indispensable in ordinary life for normalizing intercourse with the extraordinary. For this reason, even postmetaphysical thinking continues to coexist with religious practice. . . . Philosophy, even in postmetaphysical form, will be able neither to replace nor repress religion as long as religious language is the bearer of a semantic content that is inspiring and even indispensable, for this content eludes (for the time being?) the explanatory force of philosophical language and continues to resist translation into reasoning discourses.[39]

Habermas literally inserts a parenthetical question into his assessment of religion in the modern world, reinforcing his assertion that we must remain open to the question of whether religious truth claims offer

---

[37] Jürgen Habermas, "Transcendence from Within, Transcendence in the World," in Eduardo Medieta, ed., *Religion and Rationality: Essays on Reason, God and Modernity* (Cambridge, MA: MIT Press, 2002), 79, emphasis in original.

[38] See Eduardo Mendieta's introduction to Jürgen Habermas, *Religion and Rationality: Essays on Reason, God and Modernity*, 1–36.

[39] Habermas, *Postmetaphysical Thinking*, 51.

something irreplaceable to rational discourse. His observation that religious truths resist translation complicates his insistence upon the need for translation of religious claims in order to enter into public discourse. In my view, Habermas lacks a coherent analysis of the nature and role of religious truth claims because he has yet to systematize religious truth into his epistemology. In other words, Habermas does not locate religious discourse in his understanding of objective truth, social rightness, or subjective authenticity, leaving us to speculate on the nature of religious validity claims. As yet, Habermas does not explicitly recognize the rational status of religious truth claims despite his multidimensional understanding of rationality. Religious truth claims are ostensibly left out of his theory of discourse; yet Habermas acknowledges the significance of religious truth on multiple levels of society. Integrating religious truth claims into his discourse theory may fill in some gaps that critics have highlighted in response to his work. In order to locate religious discourse within Habermas's framework of communicative rationality, I will now analyze his understanding of discourse and highlight limitations of his theory to address religious discourse by turning to feminist critiques of Habermas's discourse ethics.

THEORETICAL, PRACTICAL, AND RELIGIOUS DISCOURSE

Habermas's theory of communicative action is dependent upon his understanding of discourse in the sense that his understanding of discourse allows him to assert that rationality is the basis for communicative action. Habermas defines rationality as follows:

> The rationality of a person is proportionate to his expressing himself rationally and to his ability to give account for his expressions in a reflexive stance. A person expresses himself rationally insofar as he is oriented performatively toward validity claims: we say that he not only behaves rationally but is himself rational if he can give account for his orientation toward validity claims.[40]

The validity claims of truth, rightness, and truthfulness remain implicit until there is a disruption in the flow of communicative action. When a disruption occurs, Habermas suggests that the participants must enter into discourse. Through discourse, validity claims are made explicit so

---

[40] Habermas, "Some Further Clarifications of the Concept of Communicative Rationality," in Cooke, ed., *On the Pragmatics of Communication*, 310.

that they may be accepted or rejected by all participants in the communicative action. In other words, we do not realize the basic agreements that allow social coordination to occur until we encounter a conflict. When a disagreement occurs, we are asked to become reflexive about our assumptions and make them explicit.

Habermas's theory of discourse also clarifies his understanding of truth, knowledge, and meaning. With the intention of rejecting both positivist and relativist models of truth, Habermas holds that validity claims emerge out of local contexts, but they can also transcend those contexts and potentially achieve universal assent. He stresses this by arguing that we arrive at publicly credible statements through the process of the intersubjective recognition of validity claims in discourse. In developing a multifaceted understanding of validity claims, he also develops a multidimensional theory of truth. Depending on its objective, social, or subjective orientation, the validity claim invites a different level of consensus for its legitimation. This allows him to talk about how statements about the social and subjective worlds can be valid or invalid in a manner analogous to true or false statements about the objective world. This challenges the positivist notion that places truth solely in the objective realm. At the same time, by arguing for the rational structure behind the validation of any type of validity claim, Habermas refutes relativist claims that we cannot arrive at truth. In his avoidance of positivism and relativism, Habermas's epistemology offers a unique and valuable perspective on the nature of religious truth claims for a postmetaphysical context. However, he does not explicitly locate religious discourse within his theory, inviting us to construct a framework for religious discourse.

In this section, I explore the nature of religious discourse within Habermas's framework. I argue that religious validity claims can appeal to all three dimensions of Habermas's framework of theoretical discourse: truth, rightness, and subjective truthfulness. Religious statements often involve some kind of claim to objective truth, which believers verify through identifying historical events as revelatory. They involve claims to rightness, offering ethical and moral guidelines to regulate the social world. Finally, religious statements appeal to the subjective realm, validated by the authenticity of an individual's religious experience. I agree with Maeve Cooke who asserts that religious discourse is unique and challenges some of the boundaries between Habermas's categories of theoretical discourse. Cooke locates religious discourse in between the contextual and the universal, arguing that religious validity claims can serve as bridges between the particular and the transcendent.[41] This makes sense in light of the fact that religious discourse is embedded in a particular tradition and also makes claims to universal significance. Habermas's discourse theory, I argue, does not adequately support the contextual and universal dimensions of religious validity claims. Therefore, it is unclear how Habermas's discourse theory can be applied to practical questions of religious discourse, such as the question of how religious claims function in ecumenical dialogue.

Scholars such as Cooke have rightfully critiqued Habermas's theory for its lack of inclusion of religious discourse.[42] Habermas recognizes different kinds of truth, arguing that a truth claim can appeal to social, objective, or subjective validation. However, Habermas's lack of attention to the particularity of religious truth claims limits his multidimensional epistemology. He has received similar critiques with regard to his limited perspective on aesthetic truth. In Habermas's debate with Gadamer, the nature of artistic truth claims was highlighted as a point of contention.[43] From the perspective of Gadamer's philosophical hermeneutics, artistic truth claims are not just expressive but disclosive. In other words, they do not simply reveal the artist's subjective reality; they also disclose a nonsubjective truth. Some scholars of religion argue that religious and artistic truth claims are analogous.[44] While I agree with the conclusion of Gadamer's hermeneutics, I do not want to argue for the same analogy between artistic and religious validity claims. Convinced that religious validity claims, which carry ethical and moral dimensions, have a critical function in society, I stay within the framework of critical theory to understand the nature of religious validity claims.

Religious truth can be integrated into Habermas's framework by drawing on feminist critiques of Habermas's discourse ethics. Critical theorists Seyla Benhabib and Maria Pia Lara challenge some of Habermas's assumptions about universality and the public/private distinction. Their

---

[41] Maeve Cooke, "Salvaging and Secularizing the Semantic Contents of Religion: The Limitations of Habermas' Postmetaphysical Proposal," *The International Journal of Philosophy and Religion* 60 (2006): 187–207.

[42] Ibid.

[43] See G. B. Madison, "Critical Theory and Hermeneutics: Some Outstanding Issues in the Debate," in Lewis Edwin Hahn, ed., *Perspectives on Habermas* (Chicago: Open Court, 2000), 463–83.

[44] David Tracy, for example, draws upon Gadamer's philosophy to argue that religious truth claims function as "classics," revealing timeless truth by surviving multiple interpretations. See Browning and Fiorenza, eds., *Habermas, Modernity and Public Theology*.

critiques create a space for religious claims in Habermas's discourse theory by blurring the boundary between the contextual and the universal and by articulating the critical function of particular narratives in the public sphere. In what follows, I outline the major features of Habermas's discourse theory, paying particular attention to his understanding of ethical and moral discourse. This will lay out a foundation for understanding feminist critiques of his perspective, which I draw upon to better understand the nature of religious discourse.

Habermas uses "discourse" as a technical term to describe the dialogical or argumentative process of reaching consensus through the explicit criticism and defense of validity claims. He states:

> I shall speak of discourse only when the meaning of the problematic validity claim conceptually forces participants to suppose that a rationally motivated agreement could in principle be achieved, whereby the phrase, "in principle" expresses the idealizing proviso: if only the argumentation could be conducted openly enough and continued long enough.[45]

As Habermas indicates here, discourse requires a presupposed "ideal speech situation" in which rationality is the sole guide of argumentation. When participants enter into discourse, they commit themselves to the possibility of reaching understanding by presenting validity claims that can be agreed upon eventually through rational argumentation. Habermas admits that this ideal is "often counterfactual," but it serves as a regulating principle for the discursive process.[46] The concept of the ideal speech situation played a more important role in Habermas's earlier work. Although he still maintains that it is an important regulative principle for discourse, he has nuanced his position through emphasizing the difference between recognizing a preexisting truth in the objective world and arriving at truth through an idealized process of discourse. Furthermore, he has pointed out that expressive truth claims do not rely on discourse for their validation but rather on a correspondence between the speaker's claim and actions.[47]

Discourse requires a level of abstraction from the context of the communication so that the nonverbals and pressures of action can be

---

[45] Habermas, *Theory of Communicative Action*, vol. 1, 42.

[46] Ibid.

[47] Jürgen Habermas, "Richard Rorty's Pragmatic Turn," in Cooke, ed., *On the Pragmatics of Communication*, 343–82.

bracketed off and the validity claims of truth, rightness, and truthfulness can become the focus of the participants. Once validity claims are made explicit through discourse, the participants must be willing to allow the force of the better—more rational—argument to motivate their mutual understanding. For Habermas, more rational arguments are the ones that can be defended with more convincing reasons. There cannot be a stra-tegic intent behind the communicative encounter, because reason must be the motivating principle of consensus. This is how Habermas argues that rationality provides the structure for the communicative action.[48]

If the force of the more rational argument is to determine the action of the communicative participants, then they must be mutually free to confirm and reject validity claims. The most basic rules of discourse guarantee the rationality behind this process. First, all participants must understand the validity claims that are raised. Second, hearers must be able to freely respond yes or no to the speakers' validity claims without coercion, self-deception, or reservation.[49] Furthermore, Habermas argues that the discourse must be inclusive of everyone affected by its outcome, and everyone must be given an equal access to the conversation.[50] This result is the goal of communicative action, namely, that mutual under-standing serves to coordinate social interaction. Habermas's rules of discourse make sense in actual contexts. Take, for example, my experi-ence at the ecumenical meeting in Belem. In order for consensus to be achieved, the discourse needed to be intelligible to all parties. For this reason, individuals would request clarification if they did not understand the conversation. The conversation itself followed rules that allowed us to approximate noncoercion and inclusivity. Each individual could object at any time, and we could not interrupt each other to move the conversation forward. In this case, one can see how the ideal of consensus created parameters around the process of discourse itself.

Habermas makes a distinction between empirical, moral, and ethical discourses and expects different levels of consensus according to the type of validity claim raised. This is highlighted in his development of discourse ethics. An ethical guideline that affects the social relationship of a particular community only requires the consensus of that community. A

---

[48] Habermas, *Theory of Communicative Action*, vol. 1, 295–304.

[49] Jürgen Habermas, "The Architectonics of Discursive Differentiation: A Brief Response to a Major Controversy," in *Between Naturalism and Religion*, 82.

[50] The principle of inclusivity and equal access is one that I will critically evaluate later in this chapter, focusing on critiques by Seyla Benhabib.

principle of justice that aims at universal significance requires a different level of consensus. How do we ever know that a moral validity claim can achieve universal significance if the discourse itself is always embedded in actual contexts? An exploration of Habermas's discourse ethics will set up the feminist critiques that I suggest are necessary in problematizing some of Habermas's assumptions about the relationship between the universal and the particular. This provides an entry into Habermas's typology of discourses that will allow for a constructive engagement on the question of the nature of religious validity claims.

Habermas distinguishes three uses of practical reason: pragmatic, ethical, and moral. Each of these employments of reason takes on a different form of discourse that has a distinct orientation. Pragmatic discourse is oriented toward the identification of effective means to a given end, ethical discourse is oriented by the question of what is good for an individual or group, and moral discourse is aimed at just action.[51] Ethical and moral questions are different from pragmatic questions in that they relate to value decisions of an individual or a group. Therefore, they require a different level of validity that goes beyond the relative preference of an individual. Pragmatic discourse is validated by the purposive choices of the subject. Ethical discourse, however, raises questions of value and meaning relating to what is good for an individual, not just what is possible or preferable. The matters of ethical discourse relate to one's self-understanding and evaluation of his or her life. This type of discourse raises the claim of authenticity or resoluteness of the individual or group.[52] Habermas makes an additional distinction between ethical-existential discourse and ethical-political discourse, each of which raises the claim to authenticity.[53] The former relates to a particular individual and aims at the authentic good of that person. The latter relates to a particular group and aims at the authentic good of that collective. Each discourse takes into consideration the particular context of the agent, whether it is an individual or a community. This context includes the values, history, traditions, and desires of that agent.

Moral discourse occurs when one examines how his or her actions relate to the interests of others. It requires a level of abstraction from one's own particular context in order to consider the interests of all people

---

[51] Jürgen Habermas, *Justification and Application: Remarks on Discourse Ethics*, trans. Ciaran Cronin (Cambridge, MA: MIT Press, 1993), 1–8.
[52] Ibid., 8–10.
[53] Ibid., 12, 16.

involved in the moral question. Moral discourse requires the subject to exercise free will in judging what is just in a given situation rather than to act out of practical interests or strong ethical preferences. While moral discourse strives to reach universal consensus, ethical discourse does not share those aims. Ethical discourse, associated particularly with the claim to authenticity, is concerned with the good life of a specific individual or community. This development in Habermas's discourse theory nuances his earlier emphasis on idealized consensus achieved through argumentation. Habermas received criticism for the counterfactual implications of his understanding of the ideal of consensus.[54]

In response to such criticisms, Habermas clarified his epistemology, replacing his earlier consensus model of truth with a revised pragmatic approach. In a commentary on Richard Rorty's radical pragmatism, Habermas argues for a model of truth that recognizes the process of justification behind every truth claim about the objective world but also recognizes that objective truth is not created by reaching consensus about it. In other words, people can come to agreement and hold something to be an objective fact that may turn out to be false. Habermas claims that objective truth functions in the background of everyday interactions, and he recognizes how truth can always be brought into question and subjected to rational critique. People have an interest in maintaining consensus about the objective world because it functions to coordinate social action. However, because we can adopt a reflexive attitude and recognize the fallibility of truth statements, they can always be problematized through discourse. Within this model, consensus serves as a regulative idea for the process of arriving at truth, but it does not establish truth itself.[55]

Habermas presents his discourse ethics as an alternative to Kantian moral philosophy that is both critical and appreciative of Kant's thought. Habermas claims to have retained the cognitivist and universalist features of Kant's thought while avoiding some of the problems of his moral philosophy. In other words, Habermas wants to defend this cognitivist and universalist approach against contextualist and expressivist approaches that err on the side of relativism.[56] Discourse ethics relies on two assump-

---

[54] For example, see the critique by Seyla Benhabib in *Situating the Self* (New York: Routledge, 1992), 26–38.

[55] Habermas, "Richard Rorty's Pragmatic Turn," in Cooke, ed., *On the Pragmatics of Communication*, 344–72.

[56] Jürgen Habermas, *Moral Consciousness and Communicative Action*, trans. Christian Lenhardt and Shierry Weber Nicholsen (Cambridge, MA: MIT Press, 1990).

tions. First, the validity claims of moral norms have a cognitive quality and can be compared analogously to truth claims. Like truth claims, we come to understand these normative "oughts" because they can be defended with good reasons.[57] Second, the justification of moral norms requires consensus achieved through rational discourse. Remembering the model of discourse from his theory of communicative action, we can understand discourse to require the explication of validity claims in order to argue for them based on reason alone.

Habermas replaces Kant's categorical imperative (i.e., something is morally acceptable if it is acceptable for everyone in that circumstance) with his "universalization principle" (U). Following the method of discourse ethics, this principle states that a moral norm is valid only if "all affected can accept the consequences and the side effects its *general* observance can be anticipated to have for the satisfaction of *everyone's* interests (and these consequences are preferred to those of known alternative possibilities for regulation)."[58] The norm is discovered either to be or not to be in everyone's interest through practical discourse. It does not necessarily claim to be universally applicable in all cases. It claims to represent the general interests of all people affected by it.

Habermas claims to pay attention to context by arguing for two necessary discourses in the process of assessing moral validity claims: the discourse of justification and the discourse of application. He highlights this process in his 1993 work *Justification and Application: Remarks on Discourse Ethics*. The discourse of justification requires an abstraction of general norms from the context in order to rationally and impartially assess them as they stand. The discourse of application requires looking at the norms in the specific context and judging their situational appropriateness. Both discourses require impartiality, Habermas argues. Impartiality should not be equated with neutrality; rather, it is to be understood as the ability to consider all viewpoints.[59]

The ability to take on all viewpoints requires a level of cognitive and moral sophistication. Habermas understands the ability to use the universalization principle and engage in discourse ethics as a product of social evolution. Following his method of approaching social evolution, Habermas supports his theory with the empirical findings of the human sciences. In this case, he uses Lawrence Kohlberg's theory of moral development

---

[57] Ibid., 56.
[58] Ibid., 65, emphases in original.
[59] Habermas, *Justification and Application*, 48.

to argue for the universal acquisition of communicative competence. Habermas argues that at the postconventional level of cognitive-moral development, we are capable of rational discourse necessary for communicative action.[60]

Habermas suggests that we need to consider both universal justice and the particularity of the good life in discerning what is socially normative. However, questions of justice must come first because they relate to universal moral principles. Furthermore, we cannot rely on the classical Aristotelian approach to the good life, because he operated out of a metaphysical framework to which modern philosophy has no recourse.[61] Habermas argues that discourse ethics, with its claim to both cognitive universality and openness to critical application, provides a way to consider both justice and the good life. Habermas sums this up:

> Discourse ethics situates itself squarely in the Kantian tradition yet without leaving itself vulnerable to the objections with which the abstract ethics of conviction has met from its inception. Admittedly, it adopts a narrowly circumscribed conception of morality. But it neither has to neglect the calculation of the consequences of actions rightly emphasized by utilitarianism nor exclude from the sphere of discursive problematization the questions of the good life accorded prominence by classical ethics, abandoning them to irrational emotional dispositions or decisions. . . . The theory of discourse relates in different ways to moral, ethical, and pragmatic questions.[62]

Habermas's U principle has been challenged at length by critical theorist Seyla Benhabib.[63] While maintaining a commitment to the possibility of universalism, Benhabib argues that Habermas's U principle is inappropriate and unnecessary. She suggests that Habermas's discourse principle (D), which he applies to ethical discourses, is sufficient in providing the necessary regulation for rational, practical discourse, since the D principle guarantees that everyone affected by the outcome of the ethical decision is able to participate freely in the validation of an ethical truth claim. She specifically argues that the U principle is redundant, as it speculates beyond actual people and contexts. Instead of acting on the basis of generalized interests, claims should be validated by the actual interests

---

[60] Habermas, *Moral Consciousness and Communicative Action*, 166–67.
[61] Habermas, *Justification and Application*, 130.
[62] Ibid., 1–2.
[63] Benhabib, *Situating the Self*, 26–38.

of the concrete other.[64] In other words, we learn about the implications of an ethical decision through our experiences in real relationships and not through an abstraction from the contextual realities of that person.

At the heart of her critique, Benhabib challenges Habermas's separation of moral issues from ethical concerns. It is a mistake, she claims, to dichotomize questions of justice from questions of the good life. This allows the discussion of rights, pertaining only to issues of justice, to be privileged over the discussion of the good life. Consequently, concerns about the good life, which include the "personal" and "domestic" spheres (domains that have been the primary concerns of women), are not taken into account.[65] Carol Gilligan offers a similar critique. Known for her criticism of Kohlberg's theory of moral development, Gilligan rejects his universalist moral theory for its inadequate attention to developmental differences between men and women.[66] Privileging the universal over the particular overlooks the fact that moral issues emerge within the contexts of real life. She accuses Kohlberg of too sharply separating justice from mutual concern and care within particular relationships. Benhabib agrees with Gilligan on this point, arguing that moral issues emerge within real relationships of mutual care and that these are just as significant as issues of justice.[67]

Benhabib is committed to the model of discourse ethics, however, and accuses Gilligan of dismissing universalist principles too precipitously. She argues that Gilligan's insights can be used to supplement a universalist perspective because questions of care and nurture can be addressed as universal moral issues.[68] Benhabib proposes the category of "interactive universalism" against Habermas's universalism. In interactive universalism, we are able to maintain a vision of the common good. This vision is achieved, however, not through the ability to take on the perspective of a generalized other but through relationship to the concrete other.[69] In her development of interactive universalism, Benhabib reveals the

---

[64] Ibid., 26–38.

[65] Ibid., 158–70.

[66] Carol Gilligan, *In a Different Voice: Psychological Theory and Women's Development* (Cambridge, MA: Harvard University Press, 1982), 18–19.

[67] Seyla Benhabib, "The Debate over Women and Moral Theory Revisited," in Johanna Meehan, ed., *Feminists Read Habermas: Gendering the Subject of Discourse* (New York: Routledge, 1995), 187–98.

[68] Benhabib, "Women and Moral Theory," 189.

[69] Benhabib, *Situating the Self*, 158–64.

connection between our social location, embedded in real relationships, and our ability to imagine universals.

Benhabib's critique of Habermas's discourse ethics offers important epistemological insights for understanding forms of discourse in critical theory. By stressing the contextual embeddedness of all our ideas, including our ideas about universality, Benhabib invites us to articulate how our social location shapes our approach to any discourse. Her critique problematizes Habermas's distinction between contextual and universal thinking, as explicitly articulated in his differentiation between ethical and moral discourse. The blurry area between contextual thinking and context-transcending truth claims, I think, is the best place to locate religious validity claims in Habermas's theory.

Religious validity claims are unique in the sense that they are undeniably grounded in a narrative of a particular community and yet often attempt to have universal significance. To offer an example from my faith tradition, Catholic social teaching claims to speak to a double audience. Particularly since the Second Vatican Council, Catholic social ethicists have acknowledged the historical and contextual nature of their claims, drawing explicitly on biblical and theological sources instead of relying solely on natural law. In light of this, they speak in a language that particularly resonates with members of that tradition. At the same time, however, they attempt to address humanity as a whole, arguing for a global common good and for universal human rights. Specifically, the teaching on the dignity of the human person is grounded in a particular biblical narrative and theological anthropology, but it claims to have implications for all of humanity.

Maeve Cooke suggests that religious validity claims offer a bridge between universal and nonuniversal truth statements.[70] She argues that Habermas's failure to recognize the uniqueness of religious truth claims leaves his discourse theory incomplete. Cooke also points out that Habermas is unable to integrate religious truth claims into his overall theory because he does not recognize the ways in which religion has responded to a postmetaphysical context. To return to the example of Catholic social teaching, one can identify a twentieth-century shift away from natural law arguments toward a more historically conscious approach. Acknowledging the ways in which religion responds to the demands of a postmetaphysical context illustrates the rational potential of religious truth claims.

---

[70] Cooke, "Salvaging and Secularizing the Semantic Contents of Religion," 192.

Along with Cooke, I think religious truth claims are in a unique position to bridge the contextualist and universalist features of Habermas's thought. In a concrete way, they provide a link between ethical-political discourse that addresses a particular community and moral discourse that claims universal significance. In so doing, they address Benhabib's critique of Habermas's private/public distinction. Furthermore, they can remind us of the contextual nature of truth claims by drawing explicitly upon a particular tradition. Locating oneself in a particular location is essential for acknowledging the limitations of one's ability to speak universally.

Understanding religious truth claims as bridges between the particular and the universal addresses the existing tension in Habermas's understanding of religion. On the one hand, Habermas recognizes the particular ability of religious discourse to address existential concerns that emerge on a lifeworld level. This function cannot be replaced—as yet, he suggests—by philosophical discourse. On the other hand, Habermas has begun to advocate for the public role of religion. In order for religious truth claims to be incorporated into public policy, however, they must be expressed in nonreligious language. It is unclear, from Habermas's proposal, how this translation process can occur. As I mentioned previously, Habermas's quandary in this area can be addressed through a better understanding of the nature of religious truth claims as both contextual and universally oriented. This can be promoted through reframing the public/private spheres in Habermas's theory of society. Critical theorist Maria Pia Lara does this in her retrieval of narrative in bridging public/private discourse. Her insights are helpful in understanding the way that religion functions on the levels of lifeworld and system.

A CRITICAL SOCIAL THEORY AND THE PUBLIC ROLE OF RELIGION

Habermas makes a case for the necessity of critical theory through his understanding of the process of rationalization in the development of modern society. As I stated previously, in the process of modernization the lifeworld is rationalized and the systems become more complex. When the lifeworld and systems become more differentiated from each other, knowledge is specialized and separated from the background knowledge of the lifeworld. This process allows systems to become independent of the lifeworld and thus detached from the immediacy of communicative action.[71] The detachment of social systems from the communicative action of the

---

[71] Habermas, *Theory of Communicative Action*, vol. 2, 318–31.

lifeworld has created the conditions for various modern social pathologies. For example, in a modern context, a health care system can be driven by the financial concerns of insurance companies more than by the medical needs of individuals. It is the task of critical theory to address such social pathologies, exposing unarticulated interests behind taken-for-granted social realities. The role of religion in aiding critical theory to address the problems of modernity is not self-evident. Is religious discourse an irrational form of social cohesion that hinders the free exchange of rational validity claims? Can religion bridge lifeworld knowledge with specialized knowledge of systems? In other words, does religion have a public voice in modern societies?

Recently, Habermas has recognized the role of religion in articulating a shared vision of the social world. Largely in response to the ethical questions raised by increased biotechnologies that have the potential of radically altering our understanding of the human person, Habermas has advocated for religion to have a public voice in global discussions on the future of humanity.[72] This is an example of religion bridging understandings of the human person that are grounded in immediate relationships (i.e., knowledge of the lifeworld) with understandings of the human person that are shaped by specialized knowledge (i.e., scientific knowledge). In order for religion to participate in the project of critical theory, it must have a public voice in society.

Habermas's contemporary perspective on religion is shaped by his understanding of the public sphere. This has been a focus of his work since the beginning of his academic career with the publication of *The Structural Transformation of the Public Sphere*. In this work he describes the rise of the bourgeois public sphere in the eighteenth century as a place where private interests could be negotiated publicly. In this context, the public space had an explicit political function, which is necessary for a democratic society. As liberal capitalism developed and the role of the media changed, the public sphere lost its critical function. Now, the media assumes a pseudopublic role of representing general interests, but political opinion has become privatized. Habermas is concerned with retrieving the critical function of the public sphere as essential to deliberative democracy.[73]

---

[72] Jurgen Habermas, *The Future of Human Nature*, trans. Hella Beister and William Rehg (Cambridge: Polity Press, 2003).

[73] Jürgen Habermas, *The Structural Transformation of the Public Sphere: An Inquiry into a Category of Bourgeois Society*, trans. Frederick Lawrence (Cambridge, MA: MIT Press, 1991), 181–235.

Habermas's theory of discursive politics provides a key insight into his understanding of the public sphere, which shapes his approach to religion. In *Between Facts and Norms: Contributions to a Discourse Theory of Law and Democracy*, Habermas defends the possibility of democracy within the complex and pluralistic context of modern society.[74] The process of law making in the framework of discursive democracy is similar to the process of ethical decision making in the framework of discourse ethics. Both models rely on cognitivist and universalist assumptions about the participants in the discourse. Participants in democratic law making must enter into discourse in which they make explicit their validity claims and allow the force of the better argument to bring them to consensus.[75] As in discourse ethics, Habermas's discourse theory of democracy follows a principle of consensus. In order for a political decision to be legitimate, it must represent the general interests of all citizens affected by its consequences. Habermas realizes that the complexity of a pluralistic society makes the ideal of consensus recognition of the common good difficult to imagine. In real-life legislative processes, compromise and majority decision making is required. However, compromise does not negate the ideal of consensus, because it is always provisional.[76]

The process of discursive decision making must be ongoing. In democratic societies, the role of the legal system is to ensure the right to ongoing, unconstrained discourse.[77] In other words, the role of the law is to protect the rights of citizens to voice their opinions publicly; law should also protect the lifeworld conditions of the social community. It does this by providing the freedom to engage in political discourse and by providing institutionalized parameters of this discourse based upon the provisional judgment of the common good. This position reflects Habermas's concern with protecting both individual freedom and the common good. Consequently, he is not opposed to legitimate institutions, but he stresses that their legitimacy is based on their ability to represent the general interest of all affected by their decisions.

Habermas recognizes the complexity of defining the common good in a pluralistic context. He has taken up the challenges posed by this complexity in his discussion of the role of religion in the secular social/

---

[74] Jürgen Habermas, *Between Facts and Norms: Contributions to a Discourse Theory of Law and Democracy*, trans. William Rehg (Cambridge, MA: MIT Press, 1996).

[75] Ibid., 38–141.

[76] Ibid., 162–68.

[77] Ibid., 38–41.

political sphere. His recent participation in these conversations reveals two theoretical commitments that are worth noting. First, he continues the Kantian insistence on the need to translate religious truth claims into ethical principles presented in secular language. Second, he recognizes the unique role of faith and religious practice in providing meaning and stability within the lifeworld. Taken together, these commitments speak to the challenge of establishing social unity within the context of religious pluralism.

Habermas's political theory is shaped by the assumption that the political sphere must provide an open forum for rational discourse. Since everyone affected by the political decisions of a given society must be able to participate in the legitimation of norms and laws, such norms and laws must reflect a generally accessible language. Religious vocabulary can be expressed on the level of the informal public sphere, which should inform the level of policy. This assumption provides the foundation for Habermas's position on the relationship between the religious and the secular. Religious truth claims have an important role in shaping social norms, but for the institutional exercise of authority they must be translated into secular language in order to be intelligible to the wider society. This does not mean that religious people should be asked to deny the connection between their approach to social/ethical norms and their personal faith commitments, as John Rawls suggests.[78] Secular thinkers are also asked to recognize the positive role of religious practice in developing social/ethical principles by observing this connection. Therefore, the translation process requires a joint effort, based on mutual respect, among religious and secular members of the society.

Habermas illustrates this in a concrete way through his recent discussions with Joseph Ratzinger on the topic of religion and secularity.[79] Habermas highlights the contributions of Christianity to the development of the Western tradition of reason. In doing so, he argues that secular thinkers should respectfully acknowledge the rationality behind

---

[78] Habermas disagrees with Rawls's argument that religious individuals need to privatize their religious values for the sake of participation in the secular sphere. While Habermas agrees with Rawls on the point that religious values need to be translated into secular language, he also maintains that religious individuals should not have to make the false separation between religious and secular commitments. The connection between secular principles and religious values should be recognized by both religious and nonreligious members of society. See Habermas, "Religion in the Public Sphere," in *Between Naturalism and Religion*, 120–24.

[79] Habermas and Ratzinger, *The Dialectics of Secularization: On Reason and Religion.*

such religious truth claims. He also highlights the relationship between Christianity and Western philosophy as an example of the real possibility of translating religious truths into secular language in order to develop social norms. Habermas's insistence upon the translation of religious truth claims into secular language has been the subject of criticism. Some theologians and scholars of religion argue that the meaning of a religious truth claim is tied to the particular narrative out of which it emerges.[80] Habermas himself has admitted that there is a loss of meaning when religious claims are translated outside of the faith community. This testifies to the inescapable contextuality of all thinking, which scholars such as Benhabib adamantly stress. The question at hand, therefore, is how a particular religious narrative can be meaningful outside of the community from which it emerges.

I have suggested, along with others, that religious discourse is unique and does not fit neatly into Habermas's schema. Understanding religious truth claims as bridges between the particular and the universal provides a way to address Habermas's public/private split, for which he has been criticized. Critical theorist Maria Pia Lara offers a way to reframe Habermas's understanding of the relationship between public and private concerns. Drawing upon Hannah Arendt's emphasis on storytelling as a way to facilitate social change, Lara suggests that narrative has an important role in creating and transforming public opinion. In her view, this is one way that the public sphere can reclaim its critical function.[81] Her main critique of Habermas is that he fails to recognize the role of culture in modern societies. This creates a bifurcation of lifeworld and system, which shapes his understanding of the public/private split. Lara argues that feminist narratives reveal the fallacy of this public/private split, as they create pathways between the private and the public. As aesthetic and political tools, feminist narratives are both expressive and emancipatory. She states:

> The basic error in Habermas's dualistic conception of system and life-world stems from its inability to conceptualize the mediation between spheres that is provided by the cultural domain, where actions reveal their connection to communicative reason in a decentered way. By

[80] This perspective is exemplified by George Lindbeck. See George Lindbeck, *The Nature of Doctrine: Religion and Theology in a Postliberal Age* (Louisville: John Knox Press, 1984).

[81] Maria Pia Lara, *Moral Textures: Feminist Narratives in the Public Sphere* (Berkeley: University of California Press, 1999), 2–11.

publicly thematizing their new identity projects, feminists have created mediations between particularistic and universal claims.[82]

Religious discourse can function in a similar way. By explicitly acknowledging the particular narrative out of which religious truth claims emerge, religious language can enter into public discourse honestly and prophetically. Returning to the example of Catholic social teaching, I would like to point out that the theological response to a postmetaphysical context has been to become more explicit about the historicity and contextuality of ideas. To translate particular narratives into secular language in order to make them more universally accessible betrays, in a sense, the postmetaphysical turn to which Habermas is so committed.

Habermas differentiates between the level of deliberation and the level of policy, leaving room for the possibility of nontranslated exchange between religious and secular people on a deliberative level.[83] However, he insists that policies must be expressed in secular language because of its universal accessibility. It is worth noting, however, that the Western secular perspective is grounded in a particular narrative as well. Therefore, it should not be assumed to be more universally accessible than a religious perspective. I am convinced by Habermas's claim that policy must reflect the individuals that it represents. However, we should not assume that secular language is universally representative. A common language should emerge out of the dialogue itself, making the need for ongoing public discourse evident. This position supports Habermas's claim that a public sphere is necessary for social solidarity in a pluralistic context.

Drawing upon Habermas's theory of communicative action, we can imagine the development of solidarity between religious and secular citizens. Habermas's general principles of discourse—namely, inclusivity, freedom to participate, honesty, and the freedom to accept or reject the validity claims of the other on rational ground—can also guide this exchange. I would add that the discourse must make room for religious validity claims by recognizing the rational potential of narrative. Through the exchange of narratives, a common language that will facilitate collaboration between religious and secular citizens may emerge. Bridging differences, especially religious differences that touch the core of one's identity, is a daunting task. The ecumenical movement, I suggest, can pro-

---

[82] Ibid., 170.
[83] Habermas, "Religion in the Public Sphere," in *Between Naturalism and Religion*, 139.

vide a model for replacing division with solidarity through the exchange of particular narratives. This model can promote unity in contexts that lack a common religious foundation.

CONCLUSION

In his theory of communicative action, Habermas provides a viable framework for dialogue across difference within a postmetaphysical context. With the rise of historical consciousness and the emphasis on real practice over abstract theories, contextual differences have become more evident than ever. Instead of ruling out the possibility of consensus across this difference, Habermas develops a way to conceptualize universality within our very capacity to communicate. Through his principles of discourse, Habermas illustrates the human potential to arrive at shared truths through honest, open, and noncoercive means. The exercise of discursive rationality has implications for the way we form social solidarity and discern what is good and just within and across particular communities.

In many ways, the postmetaphysical context to which Habermas responds is analogous to the ecumenical situation today. Ecumenists search for solidarity and common action within the reality of pluralism. The positive value of difference is recognized as we seek unity in such a way that does not privilege one vision of unity over another. Habermas's theory of communicative action, expanded by critical readings of his discourse theory, provides theoretical and practical insights into this ecumenical challenge.

Exploring the implications of Habermas's thought for the ecumenical movement provides insight into an underdeveloped area of his work. The nature of religious truth claims and the role of these claims in a postmetaphysical context is, for Habermas, an important topic. The ecumenical context frames this topic around the question of procedure rather than of definition. The debates around the rationality of metaphysical truth claims exist within and outside of religious communities. A uniform answer should not be desired, as it is not possible. Rather, this situation invites an approach to dialogue that can sustain the search for understanding, consensus, and truth.

2

Ecumenical Lessons from History

The modern ecumenical movement is relatively new within the history of Christianity. Ecumenists generally identify the onset of the modern ecumenical movement in the nineteenth century when Christian missionaries began looking for ways to collaborate more effectively across denominational lines. Church divisions were more pronounced in a missionary context, inviting the churches to examine what it meant to witness to Christianity together. The First World Missionary Conference in Edinburgh (1910) marks, in a particular way, the beginning of the twentieth-century ecumenical movement. Kenneth Scott Latourette suggests that "Edinburgh 1910 summed up and focused much of the previous century's movement for uniting Christians in giving the Gospel to the world."[1]

While the modern ecumenical movement has its origins in the missionary context, efforts toward reestablishing or realizing Christian unity preceded the nineteenth century. In the first century, St. Paul responded to divisions within the early Christian community by exhorting the church of Corinth to regard themselves as the Body of Christ. In the sixteenth century, Desiderius Erasmus tried to heal the divisions of the Reformation by inviting Christians to consider the church as the seamless garment of Christ.[2] History offers important ecumenical principles that are still applicable today. For instance, ecumenical leaders still draw upon Paul's

---

[1] Kenneth Scott Latourette, "Ecumenical Bearings of the Missionary Movement and the International Missionary Council," in Ruth Rouse and Stephen Neill eds., *A History of the Ecumenical Movement 1517–1948* (Philadelphia: Westminster Press, 1967), 355.

[2] Desiderius Erasmus, "De Sarcienda Ecclesiae Concordia," trans. and ed., R. Himelick, in *Erasmus and the Seamless Coat of Jesus* (Lafayette, IN: Purdue University Press, 1971), 29–98.

letter to the Corinthians to encourage Christians to regard themselves as the one Body of Christ.[3]

At the same time, history reveals ecumenical efforts that ultimately failed to promote lasting unity. Shaped by multiple overlapping desires—political, cultural, personal—these efforts to promote Christian unity attest to the need for critical theory to expose how our interests shape even our well-intended initiatives to promote Christian unity. Critically analyzing these examples can also teach us some important lessons for the modern ecumenical movement. In this chapter, I have selected two historical case studies that highlight some problematic approaches to Christian unity. The first one comes from the fifth century in the aftermath of the Council of Chalcedon when postconciliar discord was dividing the church. Emperor Zeno stepped in and made an attempt to reconcile the churches, issuing his *Henoticon* in 482. The second case takes us to the fifteenth century's Council of Florence where the Eastern and Western churches made an attempt to heal the ongoing rift between them.

Applying the methodology developed in chapter 1 to these specific contexts, I hope to achieve two things. First, it will demonstrate the applicability of Habermas's theory of communicative action to real ecumenical questions. As I suggested in chapter 1, Habermas's often abstract theoretical perspective needs to be contextualized in real-life situations in order to be more intelligible and relevant. The application of Habermas's theory also highlights the appropriateness of some of the critiques of Habermas that I drew upon in chapter 1, as it demonstrates the need to account for the limitations of reason. Specifically, one can observe in actual cases the ways in which cultural narratives and power imbalances complicate the exchange of rational validity claims through discourse. By providing an analysis of these historical examples, I hope to make a case for a critical reflection on the methodology of ecumenical dialogue, which the final chapters will provide.

These case studies reveal how the attitudes and assumptions of the participants in the ecumenical encounter shape the outcome of their efforts. They also highlight how power dynamics impact the way in which the goal of the ecumenical effort is framed and approached, inviting us to employ ways to minimize the effects of such imbalances. A critical analysis of Emperor Zeno's *Henoticon* and of the Council of Florence instructs

---

[3] For example, the Second Vatican Council's Decree on Ecumenism, *Unitatis Redintegratio*, refers to St. Paul's usage of the image of the Body of Christ as a foundational principle for Catholic ecumenism (UR 2).

contemporary ecumenists that (a) the goal of mutual understanding should precede additional goals in the ecumenical encounter, (b) differences as well as commonalities need to be recognized and brought into conversation, (c) dialogue must be built on a foundation of mutual respect, which allows for an honest exchange of truths, and (d) the truth claims raised by participants in the ecumenical encounter must adequately reflect the context that they are representing.

ZENO'S HENOTICON

The circumstances surrounding the composition of Emperor Zeno's edict of 482, which would become known as the *Henoticon*, are complex. When Zeno instructed Acacius, the patriarch of Constantinople, to write the edict, the emperor's political motivations arguably outnumbered any theological motivations. This is unfortunate in light of the numerous theological challenges that needed to be addressed in that historical moment. During the aftermath of the Council of Chalcedon, christological disputes had divided the churches between those who accepted the ecumenical council and those who rejected it. What could have served to clarify the christological differences and promote understanding among the churches only led to more confusion and animosity between the Chalcedonian and the non-Chalcedonian churches. Zeno's *Henoticon* ultimately failed in its aim to promote Christian unity, and the division between these churches would persist until only recently. Contemporary ecumenical work has led to greater, but not full, unity between the Oriental Orthodox (so-called Monophysite) churches and the Latin and Byzantine (so-called Dyophysite) churches.[4]

Discord over the Council of Chalcedon was precipitated by christological differences that existed between two of the five major patriarchates of the time: Antioch and Alexandria. Out of these patriarchates emerged two schools of thought related to the way in which the two natures and single personhood of Christ was theologically framed. Heresies emerging out of both schools occasioned the calling of the Council at Chalcedon in 449. Nestorius of the Antiochene school asserted that Mary was not the Theotokos, or God bearer, fueling the heretical teaching that the divinity and humanity of Jesus were distinct to the point of being separate.

---

[4] For an introduction to the ecumenical work that has been done between these churches, see Jeffrey Gros, Eamon McManus, and Ann Riggs, eds., *Introduction to Ecumenism* (New York: Paulist Press, 1998), 157–63.

Eutyches of the Alexandrian school emphasized the single personhood of Christ to the point of denying his humanity and affirming only his divine nature. It is important to note that these heresies do not represent the theological positions of the Antiochene and Alexandrian schools. However, the controversies surrounding the heresies bred animosity between the patriarchates.[5]

Cyril of Alexandria vehemently opposed Nestorianism and encouraged Pope Leo to excommunicate Nestorius on the grounds of heresy. Pope Leo also condemned Eutyches of the Alexandrian school in his *Tome* of 449. Many Alexandrians feared that Leo's *Tome* was too Nestorian in its assertion of the two natures of Christ, and they wanted to emphasize the christological position of Cyril at a council. Patriarch Dioscorus of the Alexandrian school called the Second Council of Ephesus, where he affirmed Cyrillian Christology. Ephesus II is referred to as the "robber council" because it was convened without the patriarch of Antioch. This event understandably perpetuated the tension between Antioch and Alexandria, necessitating the intervention of an ecumenical council.[6]

The Council of Chalcedon (449–51) condemned both Nestorius and Eutyches, defended Pope Leo's *Tome*, and deposed Patriarch Dioscorus. This did not resolve the christological disputes, however, and tension remained between the two schools of thought. The majority of the churches in Egypt and Syria rejected Chalcedon in the interest of defending Cyrillian Christology, while Rome and Constantinople defended the council and Leo's *Tome*. Emperor Basilicus condemned the Council of Chalcedon in an encyclical that was rejected by the pope and the patriarch of Constantinople. As one can imagine, the division between the pro-Chalcedonian churches and the anti-Chalcedonian churches threatened the unity of Christians throughout the empire.[7]

Christian unity was tied to political stability ever since Constantine's conversion in 312. This event, which gave Christians the freedom to worship in the Roman Empire, also changed the way that Christian unity would be understood in that era. Christian unity became the prerogative of

---

[5] *Zeno's Edict*, trans. A. Grillmeier, *Christ in Christian Tradition*, vol. 2.1 (Atlanta: John Knox Press, 1975). Additional commentary and historical background for this section taken from W. C. H. Frend, *The Rise of Christianity* (Philadelphia: Fortress Press, 1984), and Richard Price and Michael Gaddis, *The Acts of the Council of Chalcedon*, 3 vols. (Liverpool: Liverpool University Press, 2005).

[6] Price and Gaddis, *The Acts of the Council of Chalcedon*, vol. 1, 29–40.

[7] Ibid., 40–50.

the emperor, who saw the church as a means of securing political stability. The great ecumenical councils that defined Christian orthodoxy were, in fact, convened by emperors. Constantine, out of concern for maintaining unity throughout the empire, ordered the meeting of the bishops at Nicaea in 325. While these councils addressed theological concerns, they certainly also served political agendas. Ecumenists Ruth Rouse and Stephen Neill suggest that

> the gravest weakness of the Church Council as an instrument of church policy was its dependence on the State. Once it was admitted that the Emperor could take a hand in enforcing the decisions of a purely ecclesiastical assembly, the spiritual independence of the Church was gravely compromised. For, if the deep doctrines of the Christian Church depend in any degree at all on human powers for their establishment, the Faith may become a matter of party politics, and a change of government may result in a change of faith, an absurdity seen many times in the Christian world since the 4th century.[8]

It is important to understand Zeno's edict within this historical context, wherein it would not be surprising that an emperor would intervene in theological disputes and try to foster Christian unity, as problematic as that reality may be.

Zeno employed Acacius to write the *Henoticon* in hopes that it would resolve the tension over Chalcedon and preserve the unity of the empire. He did not explicitly take sides in the document, allowing each camp to interpret the edict in defense of its own theological position. The *Henoticon* did not condemn Leo's *Tome* or the Alexandrians. Zeno's criticism of Leo's *Tome* was subtle enough to be supported by the Antiochenes who claimed it and by the Alexandrians who rejected it. The edict also applauded Cyril of Alexandria for his faithfulness and orthodoxy, while explicitly condemning both Nestorius and Eutyches. It does not condemn Chalcedon, but it also avoids explicit reference to it, avoiding the language of "two natures" to avoid conflict with the Cyrillian supporters.[9]

The *Henoticon* appeals to the common foundation of the Christian tradition, emphasizing sameness over the differences that were causing conflict. Stressing the authority of the Nicene-Constantinopolitan Creed, the text states:

---

[8] Rouse and Neill, eds., *History of the Ecumenical Movement*, 12.
[9] Grillmeier, *Christ in Christian Tradition*, vol. 2.1, 254–56.

> Considering the source and the constitution and the power and the
> invincible shield of our Empire as the only right and true faith, which
> through divine intervention the 318 holy Fathers, assembled in Nicaea,
> expounded and the 150 holy Fathers, convened similarly in Constan-
> tinople, confirmed, . . . we and the most holy orthodox Churches
> everywhere neither have held nor hold nor shall hold nor know any-
> one who holds another creed or teaching or definition of faith or faith
> save the aforesaid holy creed of the 318 holy Fathers, which the said
> 150 holy Fathers also confirmed, and if anyone should hold such, we
> consider him an alien.[10]

Notice that the text emphasizes the authority of what the churches
agreed upon, namely, the councils of Nicaea and Constantinople. None
of the disputing churches argued about the authority of Nicaea and
Constantinople. The text takes a safe approach and avoids explicit reference to the teachings of the Council of Chalcedon in hopes of avoiding
controversial reception. The *Henoticon* neither praises the Council of
Chalcedon nor condemns it, but rather uses the occasion to stress the
orthodoxy of the Creed over any additions or omissions that may have
occurred after Constantinople. The text states:

> These things we have written, not devising a new faith, but fully as-
> suring you. But every person who had thought or thinks anything else,
> either now or at any time, either in Chalcedon or in any synod whatever,
> we anathematize, especially the aforesaid Nestorius and Eutyches and
> the persons who are of their mind.[11]

In short, the *Henoticon* affirmed what was already held in common.
Both sides of the debate rejected the heresies of Nestorius and Eutyches,
carefully avoiding any association with them. Both sides maintained the
authority of the Nicene-Constantinopolitan Creed. The question about
the legitimacy of Chalcedon was not answered in this text. Rather, it was
glossed over, perhaps intentionally, to minimize its significance within
the context of the shared faith expressed in the Creed. Consequently,
Zeno's attempt to express neutrality between the pro-Chalcedonian and
the anti-Chalcedonian churches only led to greater confusion because
both sides of the debates could use the text to support their position.

In his commentary on the text, Aloys Grillmeier identifies at least
four interpretations of the *Henoticon*. Some anti-Chalcedonian churches

---

[10] *Zeno's Edict*, trans. A. Grillmeier, in *Christ in Christian Tradition*, vol. 2.1, 252–53.
[11] Ibid., 253.

were moderate supporters of the *Henoticon* because they did not see it as rejecting the council altogether, but they point out that it does diminish the importance of the council in light of the authority of the Nicene-Constantinopolitan Creed. There were also anti-Chalcedonian churches that rejected the *Henoticon* because it did not explicitly condemn the Council of Chalcedon. Some supporters of Chalcedon supported the *Henoticon* and tried to make connections between the edict and the teachings of the council. They could point out that the *Henoticon* uses the language of consubstantiality, which could be understood as a subtle reference to Chalcedon. There were also radical supporters of Chalcedon who rejected the *Henoticon* as an unnecessary compromise text.[12]

Ultimately, the *Henoticon* fueled the conflict over Chalcedon and failed to facilitate greater understanding between the pro-Chalcedonian and the anti-Chalcedonian churches. In the aftermath of its promulgation, the three patriarchs of Constantinople got caught in the middle of a conflict between the pope, the emperor, and the eastern patriarchates. Leo's successor, Pope Simplicius, did not explicitly reject the *Henoticon*, but he did excommunicate its author, Acacius. This exacerbated the division between Rome and Constantinople, which would continue under Pope Galasius I, who sided with the emperor against the patriarch of Constantinople. The synods following the *Henoticon*, including the Synod of Sidon, the Oriental Synod, and the Synod of Antioch, all found the *Henoticon* to be ineffective in facilitating Christian unity.[13]

Grillmeier describes the *Henoticon* as an "ecumenical experiment" that ultimately failed.[14] It is not difficult to see why the *Henoticon* failed to create understanding: it did not clarify anyone's position. Zeno's attempt to accommodate everyone's interests led to greater confusion, as the *Henoticon* was used to justify multiple agendas. This "ecumenical experiment" provides important lessons for the promotion of Christian unity today. For one thing, it reminds us that maintaining lasting peace does not result from glossing over real differences or ignoring the conflict that is there. Zeno's political motivation to preserve unity in the empire superseded any theological or ecclesial demands. This prohibited honest dialogue about the christological tensions that existed. Furthermore, the text itself was created by one individual under the direct authority of the emperor. The conclusions of the text did not emerge out of dia-

---

[12] Grillmeier, *Christ in Christian Tradition*, 258–63.
[13] Ibid., 270–82.
[14] Ibid., 236, 317.

logue among representatives of the communities involved; therefore, it should come as no surprise that the text was not received well by those communities. Many of the aforementioned reasons for the failures of the *Henoticon* are obvious. A more focused analysis using the insights of contemporary critical theory highlights some of the more subtle problems with this misguided effort in ecumenism.

In Zeno's attempt to reunite the churches after the Council of Chalcedon with his *Henoticon*, one can observe the problem with trying to accommodate all perspectives without truly articulating any of them. Motivated by a desire to maintain unity throughout his empire, Zeno ordered the drafting of an edict that would appease conflicting parties. In his pragmatic effort to bring the churches together, he avoided highlighting theological differences in their perspectives, thus enabling each side to interpret the document in support of their interests. This misguided attempt to promote Christian unity reminds us that intentional ambiguity does not help in the efforts to arrive at a common understanding.

I am convinced by Habermas's assertion that the inherent telos of language use is mutual understanding. Any other goal of a communicative encounter must be secondary to this fundamental intention. This is illustrated through the fact that in order for an additional goal of communication to be realized, one must establish first and foremost a basic understanding of what is being communicated. Habermas takes this basic realization and identifies an important distinction between action aimed at mutual understanding and action aimed at another goal. Again, communicative action occurs when participants coordinate their encounter around the shared goal of mutual understanding. Strategic action occurs when a speaker uses language to serve an additional goal, which may not be disclosed to the hearer. Strategic action is problematic because it prohibits the free exchange of truth claims that allows for dominance free coordination. Strategic action involves bargaining, manipulation, or even coercion between communicators.[15]

How does Habermas's distinction between communicative and strategic action inform an interpretation of the events surrounding Zeno's *Henoticon*? First, one can point out the fact that Zeno's primary goal was not the facilitation of understanding but the stabilization of the empire through the maintenance of Christian unity. One can also observe how

---

[15] Jürgen Habermas, "Actions, Speech Acts, Linguistically Mediated Interactions, and Lifeworld," in Maeve Cooke, ed., *On the Pragmatics of Communication* (Cambridge, MA: MIT Press, 1998), 220–27.

this goal shaped his approach. Zeno seems to have assumed that if he had the support of every side of the debate, the common allegiance would solidify Christian unity in a way that the Council of Chalcedon did not. This is evidenced in his emphasis on what the two sides had in common, namely, the councils of Nicaea and Constantinople. At the same time, he downplayed the areas of discord and did not address the christological differences between the Alexandrian and Antiochene schools of thought.

The result of this effort was greater division because the prerequisite of mutual understanding was not in place, making this communicative encounter more confusing than enlightening. One cannot agree with a perspective unless one has a minimal understanding of that perspective. Because Zeno's political agenda directed the effort, the *Henoticon* did not serve to clarify any theological differences, nor did it bring the perspectives together in a meaningful way, because it did not help the churches to understand the perspective of the other.

Zeno could have embraced the opportunity to focus the debate around the theological issues and to help the churches move forward to a common understanding. This would have required him to identify the points of dispute within the document. He did well to stress what the churches had in common, referring to the Nicene-Constantinopolitan Creed as the touchstone for further conversations. However, he did not lift up the details of the christological controversy. This would have necessitated an acknowledgment of the nuances that shaped the Alexandrian and Antiochene perspectives by listening to individuals that held these positions. Providing the space for each school of thought to articulate their understanding and to hear the other side would have created the opportunity for honest dialogue to begin.

In his discourse theory, Habermas suggests that we are always raising truth claims in a given communicative encounter. Providing a pragmatic analysis of language, Habermas is interested in identifying what we *do* with language. Habermas's argument hinges on the assumption that in every speech act, we raise a claim that can be verified or rejected by the response of the hearer. When the hearer validates the truth claim of the speaker, he or she responds accordingly. The truth claim, in effect, has some impact on the social relationship between the communicators.[16]

---

[16] See Maeve Cooke's introduction to Jürgen Habermas, *On the Pragmatics of Communication*, 1–19.

Informed by this discourse theory, I would like to point out that in order for the hearer to respond yes or no to the claim being raised by the speaker, the claim must first be understood. In everyday communication, claims are raised and validated without having to make the process of discourse explicit. However, when communication breaks down or understanding is lost, the speaker must make his or her truth claim explicit so that the hearer can choose to accept its validity or not. This requires a level of transparency in the process of exchanging truth claims. The hearer must be free to say yes or no to the claim and must know what he or she is affirming or rejecting. This requires honesty from the speaker and a commitment to the process of communication from both participants. Habermas suggests that "The aim of reaching understanding [*Verständigung*] is to bring about an agreement [*Einverständnis*] that terminates in the intersubjective mutuality of reciprocal comprehension, shared knowledge, mutual trust, and accord with one another."[17]

In the case of the *Henoticon*, the commonly held assumptions of Christianity were in question because of the christological controversy. This necessitated an intervention to facilitate understanding. One of the problems in this particular case was that the truth claims in dispute were not made explicit through discourse. The speakers who held the claim were not given the opportunity to articulate their truth. Zeno's intervention presented each side without really acknowledging anyone's perspective. Thus, no truth claims were raised, so nobody could validate or reject them. This encounter does not provide an example of effective discourse for several reasons. There was no free exchange of truth claims, because participants were not able to represent themselves and articulate their claims. Participants could not have reached shared knowledge or mutual understanding, because their differences were not acknowledged. If representatives from the Alexandrian and Antiochene schools could have entered into the process of discourse with a commitment to the process of reaching understanding, the encounter may have been more successful.

The action of Zeno surrounding the Council of Chalcedon reveals the complexity of negotiating unity in diversity. It offers a concrete example of how power can be used strategically to articulate a common position. Without the foundation of mutual understanding, the achieved commonality can be short lived. In the case of ecumenism, this means that

---

[17] Jürgen Habermas, "What is Universal Pragmatics?" in Cooke, ed., *On the Pragmatics of Communication*, 23.

church union that is negotiated through manipulation does not create lasting unity. This point is further evidenced in the case of the Council of Florence, to which I will now turn.

THE COUNCIL OF FLORENCE

It is important for ecumenists to know the story of the Council of Florence. Not only does it offer lessons for ecumenical dialogue, cautioning us not to repeat the mistakes of history, it also continues, for many individuals, to inform the relationship between the Eastern and Western churches. Jeffrey Gros, Eamon McManus, and Ann Riggs write, "The Eastern churches have a keen sense of remembrance, particularly in reference to Western aggression, and in some cases a sense of superiority in their confidence of apostolic fidelity." [18] Considering this observation that history plays a key role in the Eastern churches' self-understanding and approach to ecumenism, the story of the Council of Florence is important to analyze. For many Eastern churches, the Council of Florence stands out as a painful memory that needs to be heard in order for healing between the churches to occur. The story of the Council of Florence, therefore, calls for thoughtful examination as ecumenists work to reconcile the Eastern and Western churches.

Like the *Henoticon* in the fifth century, the Council of Florence in the fifteenth century provides an example of misguided ecumenical efforts by individuals in positions of power. Also like the *Henoticon*, this case study offers lessons for what not to do in ecumenical dialogue. In the case of the Council of Florence, we are reminded that church unity cannot be achieved through coercion or manipulation. Ecumenical dialogue must be grounded in openness, freedom, and respect for the dialogue partner. The Council of Florence ultimately failed to promote reconciliation and unity between the Eastern and Western churches because it lacked this foundation. As in the case of the *Henoticon*, theological issues were clouded by sociopolitical realities. The participants of the Council of Florence were coming from different social, political, and economic contexts. These respective contexts shaped the way that the Eastern and Western churches participated in the council.[19]

---

[18] Gros et al., *Introduction to Ecumenism*, 154.

[19] See Joseph Gill, *Personalities of the Council of Florence* (Oxford: Basil/Blackwell, 1964), and John Meyendorff, *The Orthodox Church: Its Past and Its Role in the World Today*, rev. ed. (New York: St. Vladimir's Seminary Press, 1996). Gill and Meyendorff express

Historians generally agree that the division between the Eastern Byzantine church and the Western Latin church was a gradual process influenced by a number of factors, only some of which were theological.[20] In other words, one cannot pinpoint a single event that marks the decisive break between the churches. The separation was largely shaped by cultural differences between Byzantium and the Latin West, out of which were created diverse expressions of Christianity. Coupled with the political tensions between Constantinople and Rome, these differences often led the churches to misunderstand and/or disregard the other as a foreign entity and not a sister church. Referring to the division between the Greek and Latin churches, Orthodox historian John Meyendorff states, "In attempting to explain the nature of the schism we are forced to admit that both theological and non-theological factors were hopelessly mixed up together."[21]

While no single event marks the beginning of the schism, one can identify some specific moments in history that had a decisive influence on the division of the Eastern and Western churches. The primary issues addressed at the Council of Florence are rooted in particular conflicts that mark the history of the church. I will discuss the two main topics that are still areas of tension today, namely, the question of Roman primacy and the issue of the *filioque* in the Creed. Focusing on these areas of discord provides an entry into a shared history that is far too complex to cover in the space of this chapter.

The five major patriarchates of the patristic world were Rome, Jerusalem, Antioch, Alexandria, and Constantinople. The jurisdiction of these patriarchates implied collegiality and equality among the patriarchs. The idea of Roman primacy developed historically and is interpreted differently by the East and the West. Leo the Great shaped the Western understanding of Roman primacy with his claim to universal jurisdiction in the fifth century. For the East, the idea of universal jurisdiction lacks any theological justification.[22] Therefore, one can imagine that the rise of papal authority in the Western church during the Middle Ages drove a wedge between the Eastern and Western churches. The crowning of

---

different perspectives on the factors that influenced the proceedings at the Council of Florence. I agree with Meyendorff, who stresses the lack of freedom on the part of the Eastern churches due to the power imbalances at the council.

[20] Rouse and Neill, eds., *History of the Ecumenical Movement*, 14–19.

[21] Meyendorff, *The Orthodox Church*, 36.

[22] Ibid., 36.

Charlemagne by the pope in 800 exemplified the assertion of Roman primacy and wedded the pope with the political authority of the time. Meyendorff suggests that this event aligned the Roman church with the Frankish kings against the Byzantine Empire, perpetuating the division between the East and the West in a decisive way.[23]

It was during the Carolingian Empire that the *filioque* likely emerged. Within the Visigothic context of Spain, missionaries likely inserted into the Nicene-Constantinopolitan Creed that the Holy Spirit proceeds from the Father *and the Son* in order to emphasize the trinitarian nature of God to distinguish Christianity from Islam. Walter Kasper explains that the *filioque* "was located in the context of a specifically Western problem, but was also recognized by the East in its objective concern."[24] We know that the Eastern missionaries Cyril and Methodius were appalled to encounter this addition to the Creed and reported back to Constantinople. This event led to the first of a series of mutual excommunications between the pope and the patriarch of Constantinople, with Pope Nicolas and Patriarch Photius and in 867.[25] The churches were reunited under Pope John, but the division was not healed. The *filioque* issue was not resolved in these conversations, as evidenced in the subsequent theological disputes precipitating the Fourth Lateran Council (1215) to declare the *filioque* as a doctrine. This event, according to Kasper, "sealed the division on the part of the West."[26]

Since the theological significance of the *filioque* was not sufficiently discussed, it is not surprising that the issue resurfaced, sparking another mutual excommunication. The *filioque* issue emerged again in 1054 when Pope Leo IX and Patriarch Michael Cerularius attempted a reunion that once again ended in mutual excommunications. Cerularius initiated a reunion with the West; however, when papal delegates arrived with an insulting letter that made demands on the Eastern church that they might "return" to the West, he questioned the authenticity of the letter (especially since the pope was in exile at the time).[27] The legates excommunicated the patriarch, who reciprocated, resulting in a schism between

---

[23] Ibid., 36–39. See also Walter Kasper, who suggests that Byzantium saw the crowning of Charlemagne as a "betrayal," in *That They May All Be One: The Call to Unity Today* (New York: Continuum / Barnes and Oates, 2004), 111.

[24] Kasper, *That They May All Be One*, 110.

[25] Rouse and Neill, eds., *History of the Ecumenical Movement*, 15–16.

[26] Kasper, *That They May All Be One*, 111.

[27] Meyendorff, *The Orthodox Church*, 47–49.

the churches. The schism may have been healed if the tragic event of 1204 had not occurred; during the fourth crusade, representatives of the Western church sacked Constantinople, leaving it even more vulnerable to Muslim invaders. This event fostered animosity between the churches and solidified the division between the East and the West.[28]

This by no means exhaustive look at the events that precipitated the Council of Florence reveals a painful past of misunderstandings as well as blatant wrongdoings that needed to be reconciled. The intention to reconcile the churches was certainly one of the motivations behind Pope Eugenius's invitation to the Eastern churches to meet at an ecumenical council. In light of the complicated social and political contexts that each church was facing, it would be difficult to identify a single intention behind the Council of Florence. The Western church was still adjusting to the unstable aftermath of the Avignon papacy and the Great Schism, which shook people's confidence in papal authority. The Eastern church was facing political instability and financial hardship as Constantinople was under Turkish invasion. It is evident that each church had nontheological reasons to reunite the churches.

Pope Martin V convened the council in Basel in accordance with the Council of Constance (1414), which had ordered that councils be held frequently in the ongoing life of the church. This was one of the stipulations laid out by the conciliarists at Constance in the document *Frequens*.[29] Additionally, Constance argued that a general council has the authority to convene without the consent of the pope and that it may assume authority over the pope to protect the church against heresy or schism, as indicated in the document *Haec sancta*.[30] The conciliarist teachings at Constance were in direct response to the Great Schism, which lasted from 1309–78. At the height of the schism, there were three claimants to the papal office: a pope in Rome, a pope in Avignon, and a pope elected at the Council of Pisa in a failed attempt to end the schism. The Great Schism challenged the understanding that the pope could guarantee unity in the church. In response, the conciliarists reconceived the pope's authority in such a way that the church, as a whole body represented in a general council, could exercise authority over the pope if he

---

[28] Rouse and Neill, eds., *History of the Ecumenical Movement*, 17.

[29] Francis Oakley, *Council Over Pope: Toward a Provisional Ecclesiology* (New York: Herder and Herder, 1969), 52.

[30] Joseph Lynch, *The Medieval Church: A Brief History* (London and New York: Longman, 1992), 332.

failed to protect the unity of the church.[31] The conciliarist influence that preceded the council is necessary to understand the dynamic between the pope and the council that had been convened at Basel. Martin V died shortly after convening the council, leaving his successor, Eugenius IV, to lead the group gathered at Basel. Following the legacy of Constance, the council at Basel was made up of many supporters of conciliarist theory. Eugenius clashed with them over issues regarding papal authority and at one point had dissolved the council. The conciliarists refused to back down and pressured Eugenius to retract his decision to dissolve the council. He did decide, however, to move the council to Ferrara in order to meet with the delegation from the East, with the intention of reuniting the Latin and Greek churches. Most of the council members remained in Basel while Eugenius moved on to welcome the Greeks in Ferrara.[32]

John VIII Paleologus, the emperor of Constantinople, lead the delegation in hopes that reunion with the West would give them the protection from the Turks that they desperately needed. Joseph II, the patriarch of Constantinople, supported the effort, desiring reunion with the West. The group that accompanied them was small in number and consisted of few theologians, with the exception of Mark of Ephesus, who was the only strong advocate for the theological position of the Eastern church.[33] In addition to being outnumbered, the Greeks faced numerous hardships at the council. The council itself was dragging along as they waited for more Western delegates to arrive, leaving the Greeks tired and anxious about the political unrest back home. Eugenius lacked the financial resources to give them the support that they needed, requiring him to move the council to Florence in order to receive funding to continue the council.[34]

Considering the social and economic factors surrounding the council, it is not surprising that the theological issues did not receive the thoughtful treatment that they deserved. The topics to be discussed included the main areas of theological discord, namely, the addition of the *filioque* in the Nicene-Constantinopolitan Creed and the question of papal primacy. The council also addressed the question of whether they should use leavened or unleavened bread in the Eucharist and how to

---

[31] Oakley, *Council Over Pope*, 74–77, and Brian Tierney, *Foundations of the Conciliar Theory: The Contribution of the Medieval Canonists from Gratian to the Great Schism* (Cambridge: Cambridge University Press), 1–6.

[32] Lynch, *The Medieval Church*, 333–35.

[33] Meyendorff, *The Orthodox Church*, 52.

[34] Gill, *Personalities of the Council of Florence*, 4–5.

frame the teaching of purgatory. The question of papal primacy, though a controversial issue between the churches to this day, was resolved fairly quickly at the Council of Florence. This should raise suspicion about the depth of conversation around the issue. The *filioque* sparked the most involved discussion, but considering the role it had played in the division between the East and the West, the quick resolution of the topic at the council merits some doubt over the long-term effectiveness of the process. In the end, the issues were resolved by repeating the Latin position, not by coming to a mutual agreement on the theological topics discussed.[35]

Considering the financial troubles and the political unrest in Constantinople, it is not difficult to speculate why theological discussions were rushed. One personality at the Council of Florence stands out for his attempt to thoroughly engage the theological debates at hand. Mark of Ephesus was one of the only participants in the council who articulated the Eastern position on the *filioque* and Roman primacy without the compromise that is reflected in the council's document, *Laetentur Coeli*, the "Decree for the Greeks." Orthodox historian, John Meyendorff identifies Mark of Ephesus as the only advocate for the Eastern perspective at the Council of Florence. To many members of the Eastern churches, he stands out as a heroic figure in history.[36]

Laetentur Coeli was one of three documents produced at the Council of Florence. Each document addressed the union of the Latin church with another church, including the Greeks (to which *Laetentur Coeli* pertains), the Armenians, and the Jacobites. The text clearly reflects the Western position on the controversial theological debates. Most notably, the document speaks to the difficult issue of the *filioque* with the following statement:

> In the name of the Holy Trinity, of the Father, and of the Son, and of the Holy Spirit, with the approbation of this holy general Council of Florence we define that this truth of faith be believed and accepted by all Christians, and that all likewise profess that the Holy Spirit is eternally From the Father and the Son and has His essence and his subsistent being both from the Father and the Son, and proceeds from both eternally as from one principle and one spiration; we declare that what the holy Doctors and Fathers say, namely, that the Holy Spirit proceeds from the Father through the Son, tends to this meaning, that by this it is signified that the Son also is the cause, according to the

---

[35] Meyendorff, *The Orthodox Church*, 51–53.
[36] Ibid., 52.

Greeks, and according to the Latins, the principle of the subsistence of the Holy Spirit, as is the Father also. And that all things, which are the Father's, the Father Himself has given in begetting His only begotten Son; without being Father, the Son Himself possesses this from the Father, that the Holy Spirit proceeds from the Son from whom He was moreover eternally begotten. We define in addition that the explanation of the words "Filioque" for the sake of declaring the truth and also because of immanent necessity has been lawfully and reasonably added to the Creed.[37]

This text gives the impression that the addition of the *filioque* into the Creed was not a significant area of disagreement, claiming that their declaration was both "according to the Greeks and according to the Latins." They do not highlight the Eastern objection but rather emphasize the common theological assumptions of both churches. The Eastern churches have consistently objected to the *filioque* for historical and theological reasons. Historically, they note that the clause was inserted into the Creed without an ecumenical council and therefore lacks the authority of the Nicene-Constantinopolitan formulation. Theologically, they argue that the *filioque* addition marks a subordination of the Spirit to the Son, leading to the West's systematic lack of attention to pneumatology. Walter Kasper describes the implications of this theological difference:

[Orthodox churches] trace the (real or supposed) subordination of the charisma to the institution, of personal freedom to Church authority, of the prophetic to the juridical, of mysticism to scholasticism, of joint priesthood to hierarchic priesthood and, finally, of Episcopal collegiality to the primacy of Rome, back to this very Christomonism and, in their conviction, the resulting oblivion of the Spirit.[38]

Similarly, one can observe in *Laetentur Coeli* the strong Latin bias in the text's treatment of papal primacy. The decree states:

We likewise define that the holy Apostolic See, and the Roman Pontiff, hold the primacy throughout the entire world; and that the Roman Pontiff himself is the successor of blessed Peter, the chief of the Apostles and the true vicar of Christ, and that he is the head of the entire Church, and the father and teacher of all Christians; and that full power was given to him in blessed Peter by our Lord Jesus Christ, to feed, rule

---

[37] "Decree for the Greeks," no. 1439, trans. Henry Denzinger, *The Sources of Catholic Dogma* (Fitzwilliam, NH: Loreto Publications, 2001), 219.

[38] Kasper, *That They May All Be One*, 97.

and govern the universal Church; just as is contained in the acts of the ecumenical Councils and in the sacred canons.[39]

Again, the text does not mention the differences in the Eastern and Western understanding of the pope. This formulation simply states the Latin position, which maintains that the Roman pontiff is the head of the universal church. The ecclesiology of the Eastern church does not accept this position. Without denying the historical significance of the bishop of Rome, they deny that the pope has universal jurisdiction over the church. The Orthodox maintain that the five patriarchates of the patristic era are equal and emphasize the conciliar structure of ecclesial authority.[40]

How could the council have possibly come to an agreement on these issues that caused so much conflict and division between the churches? While historians may disagree on the level of coercion that was exercised at the council,[41] it is clear that the text of *Laetentur Coeli* reflects the Latin church's position and does not present any theological objections from the Eastern position. We know that the Latin church made up a striking majority of the voting members of the council, which caused concern regarding the voting method of the council.[42] Not surprisingly, Mark of Ephesus opposed the document and so did one Eastern bishop. The rest of the Greek delegation signed the decree, declaring their acceptance of the formulation in the text.[43] However, the teachings of *Laetentur Coeli* were not received by the Eastern church, nor were they integrated into their doctrine and practice. Ultimately, the "success" of the Council of Florence was a failure in that it did not achieve lasting unity between the Eastern and Western churches. It did not resolve the *filioque* issue, nor did it solve the question of papal primacy. Conflicts over these theological topics have persisted to this day.

---

[39] "Decree for the Greeks," in Denzinger, *Sources of Catholic Dogma*, 220.

[40] Meyendorff, *The Orthodox Church*, 189–95.

[41] From an Orthodox perspective, John Meyendorff stresses the lack of freedom behind the Greeks' participation in the council. He interprets the Council of Florence as an example of the Latin church manipulating the Eastern churches through political and economic advantage. Historian Joseph Gill, for example, recognizes the problematic aspects of the Council of Florence that impeded the freedom of the Greeks. However, he argues that they were ultimately free to sign the agreement, and he notes that only Mark of Ephesus was opposed to the decree. See Gill, *Personalities of the Council of Florence*, 14, and Meyendorff, *The Orthodox Church*, 52.

[42] Gill suggests that it is inconclusive how they reached a decision about voting. See Gill, *Personalities of the Council of Florence*, 241.

[43] Ibid., 241.

So, what does the Council of Florence have to teach ecumenists today? Some of the lessons from this attempt to create Christian unity are patently obvious. Authentic agreement does not emerge out of desperation and dependence on the other. The theological agenda of the council was not as pressing as the political and economic hardships that the participants were facing. In a particular way, the delegates from the East were overshadowed by the political duress at home. One can imagine that the safety of their families was on the forefront of their minds, leaving theological considerations in the background. Furthermore, the Eastern delegates were significantly outnumbered by the West. The Council of Florence was not set up to be a meeting of equals. It is not surprising that the Western agenda dominated the discussions because the Eastern representations paled in comparison.[44]

The Council of Florence raises questions about the possibility for a minority voice to speak their truth against the dominant majority. For many reasons, the Eastern delegates were at a disadvantage at the council. Despite the fact that they signed the decree, the teaching of the council was never received in their church because it did not reflect the authentic teaching of their church. Whether or not the West intentionally coerced the East into signing the text, the power imbalance created conditions that did not support the free exchange of positions.

I present this case study to stress the need for church unity to be born out of free and honest dialogue. If a church is prohibited, overtly or not, from speaking the truth of their tradition, honest dialogue cannot be facilitated. Furthermore, I argue that the Council of Florence reminds us that representatives of a particular tradition must be held accountable to those whom they represent. I am not implying that the Greek delegates at the council were given a fair opportunity to represent the position of their church, but it should impress upon ecumenists today the need for church agreements to emerge organically from the churches involved if they are to be received in those churches. If church leaders/representatives do not adequately represent the faith of their churches, the unity achieved in the dialogue will likely not impact the actual practices of the churches.

The example of the Council of Florence invites us to consider how the conditions of a communicative encounter impact the potential for a free exchange of truth claims between participants. As noted earlier, the Council of Florence provides a striking example of how nontheological

---

[44] John Meyendorff suggests that the Greeks were not only outnumbered but also pressured by "moral and financial pressures." See Meyendorff, *The Orthodox Church*, 52.

factors shaped the outcome of a council. Political instability and economic hardship played a decisive role in the motivation to call the council and in shaping the way that the council was approached. The pope wanted to reunite with the East to regain credibility in the eyes of the Western church during the aftermath of the Great Schism.[45] With the Turkish invasion of Constantinople, the East was desperate for support from the West. Each church had nontheological reasons for entering into the council; however, the impact of these reasons on the outcome of the council were not necessarily equally distributed. Recalling that the Eastern representatives were away from home and preoccupied with the threats of war that their families were facing, one can point out that the delegates from the East had more reasons to compromise than the West. Furthermore, it is important to note the disparity in representation at the council. All of these conditions should make one question the possibility of freedom at the council.

Using Habermas's principles of discourse, which assert that discourse must be both inclusive and dominance-free, I would like to point out that the approach to dialogue at the Council of Florence is highly problematic. For communicative action to occur, agreement must be freely achieved through discourse, allowing rationality to be the binding force of social cohesion. Habermas states:

> Processes of reaching understanding aim at an agreement that meets the conditions of rationally motivated assent (*Zustimmung*) to the content of an utterance. A communicatively achieved agreement has a rational basis; it cannot be imposed by either party, whether instrumentally through intervention in the situation directly, or strategically through exerting influence on the decisions of one party on the basis of a calculation of success. Agreement can indeed objectively be obtained by force but what comes to pass *manifestly* through outside influence or the use of violence cannot subjectively count as agreement. Agreement rests on common *convictions*.[46]

Applying Habermas's criteria for effective communicative action offers one explanation as to why the Council of Florence failed to achieve agreement on the basis of common convictions. Although agreement was made on a superficial level, it did not rest upon the free assent to the

---

[45] Gill, *Personalities at the Council of Florence*, 4.

[46] Habermas, "Social Action, Purposive Activity and Communication," in Cooke, ed., *On the Pragmatics of Communication*, 120, emphases in original.

truth claims of the other. This offers, I think, a viable argument for why the unity achieved at Florence was short lived and why, ultimately, this is an example of a poor approach to ecumenical dialogue.

Habermas states that "action coordination in general serves the purpose of social integration of a lifeworld shared intersubjectively by its members."[47] Recall from chapter 1 that Habermas considers the lifeworld to be the shared background of unthematic, taken-for-granted knowledge that a community draws upon in every communicative encounter. One of the features of the lifeworld, according to Habermas, is the immediacy of its social cohesion.[48] The most immediate form of social cohesion experienced on the level of the lifeworld is based on commonly held convictions and is reproduced by communicative action. Strategic action can also create social cohesion, but it is not the same as the social integration experienced in the lifeworld. Habermas argues that modern societies are held together through two types of social cohesion, the immediate social integration of the lifeworld and the less immediate systems integration that is facilitated by institutions. He argues that the immediate social integration that is experienced in the lifeworld should inform the systems so to avoid the "colonization of the lifeworld," which leads to alienation and loss of meaning.[49]

What does this reflection on the relationship between lifeworld and system have to do with ecumenical dialogue? For one thing, Habermas is helpful in pointing out different levels of social unity that can be experienced. The social integration that is experienced in the lifeworld is more substantial and lasting because it is grounded in shared truth claims. The truth of the lifeworld resonates with the individuals that participate in it. Similarly, one can suggest that the shared truth of one's faith tradition provides a strong experience of community that unifies the participants in that community. This is the kind of unity that ecumenism seeks to promote among Christians, one that is grounded in an immediate experience of common truth. This can be distinguished from the kind of social cohesion that occurs on the level of systems, which is removed from

[47] Habermas, "Actions, Speech Acts, Linguistically Mediated Interactions and Lifeworld," in Cooke, ed., *On the Pragmatics of Communication*, 247.

[48] See ibid., 245, where Habermas argues that three attributes of lifeworld knowledge are "immediacy, totalizing power and holistic constitution."

[49] Jürgen Habermas, *The Theory of Communicative Action*, vol. 2, *Lifeworld and System: A Critique of Functionalist Reason*, trans. Thomas McCarthy (Boston: Beacon Press, 1987), 153, 305.

the immediacy of the lifeworld. This kind of unity is less stable because it is dependent on the participants constantly affirming the legitimacy of the system's authority. When the system fails to speak to the truth of the community, it can no longer serve to coordinate that community. This kind of social cohesion can be present in the institutional level of the church. If the institutional representatives of the community do not reflect the truth claims of that community, one can expect a problem of social integration to be experienced.

In the case of the Council of Florence, the representatives of the communities in conversation did not adequately raise the truth claims of their community. There are many reasons for why this did not occur at the council. For one thing, the East lacked representation, and for another thing, nontheological factors circumvented the agenda of the encounter. The discussion of theological truth claims was not the top priority of everyone at the council. Without really engaging in the questions that emerged at the lifeworld level of the churches, the unity that was achieved at the council remained at the institutional level. Since theological truth claims were not discussed, nothing was really resolved at the council, and the compromise that was made in the decree was not received by the Eastern church. Declaring something to be true on an institutional level is subject to the community's validation of it. In the case of Florence, even though unity was "achieved" on an institutional level, it could only gain legitimacy from the communities that it claimed to represent.

Habermas's discourse theory assumes that rationality has an emancipatory effect on social integration. He argues that people are free to accept or reject a truth claim inasmuch as they are free to embrace the most rational argument. As noted in the first chapter, Habermas's notion of rationality is multidimensional and intersubjective, avoiding some of the problems with the Enlightenment model of disembodied, subject-centered reason. However, critics have rightly pointed out the problems behind the assumption that, first of all, reason is emancipatory and, second, the most rational argument brings us closer to shared truth. As noted in the previous chapter, critical theorists such as Seyla Benhabib and Maria Pia Lara are helpful in pointing out some of the limitations in Habermas's theory while maintaining a commitment to communicative rationality.

In this case, Lara is helpful in pointing out that narrative can also serve the emancipatory function of Habermas's conception of reason, as it has a transformative effect on the community. Highlighting how feminist narratives are at the same time aesthetic and political, Lara breaks down Habermas's distinction between expressive and normative truth claims.[50] Lara describes the goal of her work as highlighting "the normative content of the public sphere and the important cultural role of emancipatory narratives that can crystallize in transformations of our self-understandings."[51] The Eastern church's ecclesial self-understanding and theological perspective is grounded in a cultural and historical narrative that was not heard at the Council of Florence. If they had been free to articulate this story, and if they had been heard at the council, the proceedings at Florence would have been different and more successful, in the sense that they could have arrived at a deeper understanding of the other, even if they could not achieve full, visible unity at the time.

The Council of Florence illustrates how multiple factors can limit an individual's freedom in a communicative encounter. We should ask whether we can imagine any speech situation in which the Eastern representatives could have freely raised truth claims and responded without reservation to the claims raised by the West. Habermas uses the principle of consensus that occurs under ideal conditions as a regulative principle for real discourse, acknowledging that the ideal conditions rarely occur. However, one could rightfully object to this idealization of consensus by pointing to the real conditions that inhibit the process of discourse.

Going back to the criticism that was voiced in response to my proposal in Belem, I would like to address the challenge of achieving dominance-free discourse within contextual realities that impede one's freedom to speak. It is helpful to refer to postcolonial theorist Gayatri Spivak here, who raises the question of whether everyone can freely speak under the real conditions of communication. Her perspective is helpful in pointing out some of the limitations in Habermas's theory of discourse in real-life contexts that are shaped by dynamics of privilege and marginalization. In her essay "Can the Subaltern Speak?" she explores the problem of representational privilege by critiquing Western feminist projects that seek to "speak to (rather than listen to or speak for) the historically muted subject of the subaltern woman."[52] Without disregarding the usefulness of feminist theory, she critiques any attempts to unlearn contextual privi-

---

[50] Maria Pia Lara, *Moral Textures: Feminist Narratives in the Public Sphere* (Berkeley: University of California Press, 1999), 68–80.

[51] Ibid., 6–7.

[52] Gayatri Spivak, "Can the Subaltern Speak?" in Patrick Williams and Laura Chrisman, eds., *Colonial Discourse and Post-Colonial Theory: A Reader* (New York: Columbia University Press, 1994), 91.

lege and speak for people who cannot speak for themselves. She argues that ultimately the subaltern cannot speak, because the categories of communication are created by the dominant group against whom they are defined as other. Any attempts to express the truth of the subaltern rely on representation by another.[53] Spivak's postcolonial perspective on the problem of representation is helpful in pointing out how the power dynamics at play in a communicative encounter can prohibit a participant to raise truth claims, consequently resulting in the dominant perspective simply validating its own truth. This is appropriate for my analysis of the Council of Florence. I am convinced that the "Decree for the Greeks" represents the Western perspective and not a consensus statement between the two churches. The documents created at the Council of Florence give evidence to a significant disparity between the Eastern and Western churches in terms of their power to speak. Using Spivak's language of subalternity is helpful in identifying the position of the Eastern church at the council. Spivak's theory cautions us against assuming that free and inclusive discourse can be achieved in oppressive conditions.

Examining the real limitations placed on the freedom of communicators is important in evaluating the applicability of Habermas's perspective. While the ideal of consensus offers regulatory principles for the process of actual discourse, Habermas recognizes that this ideal is often counterfactual. For this reason, he argues that discourse must be ongoing. Any consensus achieved through discourse is ultimately provisional and therefore subject to the criticism of a more rational truth claim. The ideal of consensus can implore us to work to achieve the conditions for honest and free communication. In the case of the Council of Florence, the ideal conditions were impossible to achieve. However, certain conditions could have been at least approximated that would have created a greater possibility for the free exchange of truth claims. For one thing, a base level of political and economic stability should have been secured before expecting to reunite the churches. In addition, representation of the Eastern and Western churches should have been more evenly distributed to promote fair communication of both perspectives. Using Habermas's theory to analyze the power dynamics and interests behind the communicative encounter is helpful, though limited, in creating a framework of accountability for future practices in ecumenism.

---

[53] Ibid., 66–111.

Like the *Henoticon*, the Council of Florence provides an example of what not to do in ecumenical dialogue. As I have pointed out, many of their mistakes confirm ecumenical wisdom that seems obvious in hindsight. Applying insights of critical theory to analyze each case study, I would now like to develop specific principles for ecumenical dialogue that can be applied in contemporary problems concerning Christian unity. These principles will guide the subsequent chapters, which construct an approach to ecumenical dialogue based on Habermas's insights.

CRITICAL PRINCIPLES FOR ECUMENICAL DIALOGUE

Examining these cases through the lens of contemporary critical theory allows for a more critical understanding of their failed attempts to facilitate Christian unity. Applying Habermas's theory of communicative action to concrete case studies also reveals the potential for a constructive Habermasian approach to ecumenical dialogue, which I will take up in the next two chapters. As a critical theorist, Habermas is interested in uncovering the motivating assumptions behind taken-for-granted knowledge. He argues that reason allows us to uncover these assumptions and ultimately frees knowledge from ideological underpinnings. Critical theory is helpful in identifying the problems with the *Henoticon* and the Council of Florence because it exposes how multiple motivations (political and economic) interacted under the umbrella of ecumenism and created challenges to successful ecumenical dialogue.

Examining the mistakes of Zeno and the Council of Florence in many ways simply affirms ecumenical principles that are widely accepted today. Even if these principles are accepted, however, they are not always employed. Using critical theory to analyze and critique actual practices of ecumenism is helpful in addressing some of the subtle ways that mistakes are made. Furthermore, making explicit the already implicit principles of ecumenical dialogue can help foster accountability in actual ecumenical practice. To summarize the work of this chapter, I would like to highlight the following principles that can be gleaned from my critical analysis of these historical case studies: (a) the goal of mutual understanding should precede additional goals in the ecumenical encounter, (b) differences as well as commonalities need to be recognized and brought into conversation, (c) dialogue must be built on a foundation of mutual respect, which allows for an honest exchange of truths, and (d) the truth claims raised by participants in the ecumenical encounter must adequately reflect the context that they are representing.

(a) The *Henoticon* reminds us that ecumenical dialogue needs to be motivated by the goal of mutual understanding. Zeno's efforts demonstrate the fact that confusion does not create lasting unity. One might argue that the goal of ecumenism is not simply mutual understanding but full, visible unity among Christians. Scholars differentiate interreligious dialogue from ecumenism by stressing that interreligious dialogue aims at understanding and appreciating others in their difference. However, since Christians already share a common foundation, the goal of ecumenism should go beyond understanding to full, visible unity. Without disputing this important distinction, I will argue that mutual understanding is a prerequisite for any movement toward the goal of Christian unity. Habermas effectively points out the necessity for a basic level of understanding prior to the achievement of an additional goal of communication. From this perspective, churches must enter into the ecumenical encounter with the intention of coming to a greater understanding of the other even if this means highlighting conflicts that exist. This insight is particularly important to consider within conversations about the nature of Christian unity, which frames the goal of ecumenism. I will explore these conversations in the next chapter, arguing that the nature of unity must be articulated dialogically rather than assumed prior to mutual understanding.

(b) Another mistake of the *Henoticon* lies in its failure to highlight the theological differences behind the church divisions. By focusing on commonality alone, Zeno missed the opportunity to facilitate dialogue that might have created lasting unity. Glossing over the existing christological controversies created more confusion among the churches and fueled the animosity between them. This is not to suggest that commonality should not also be established in an ecumenical encounter. Recognizing the shared baptism and apostolic faith that exists among all Christians provides an important foundation for ecumenical work. The recognition of a common base, however, should provide a springboard for dialogue about the differences that exist.

Interestingly, many of the divisions between Chalcedonian and non-Chalcedonian churches have been healed as a result of carefully articulating a common Christology. The World Council of Churches identifies the "Christological method" of ecumenical dialogue as one that identifies what the churches can say together about Christ and works to formulate new language and theological frameworks that move beyond past divisions.[54]

---

[54] Gros et al., *Introduction to Ecumenism*, 120.

Key to the success of the christological method is that it allows churches to articulate a common theology together, without assuming it prior to discourse. This situation points to the need for the honest exchange of truth claims through discourse. When there is a breakdown in communicative action, or when commonly held truths cease to create social integration, communicators must enter into the process of discourse, which involves the free exchange of truth claims. Commonality is discovered or reestablished through an interactive process. I would like to argue that ecumenical dialogue, at its most effective, conforms to Habermas's basic principles of discourse.

(c) Habermas's basic principles of discourse, which foster inclusivity, equal access to the conversation, and noncoercion, are blatantly contradicted in the case of the Council of Florence. This attempt to create unity was ultimately unsuccessful because it did not allow a free and equal exchange of truth claims. Considering all of the social, economic, and political factors that impeded the freedom of participants in the council, the church-dividing issues were largely ignored, allowing the majority voice to override any dissent. The Council of Florence reminds us that ecumenical dialogue must rest on a foundation of mutual respect. Unity is not born out of manipulation and compromise to the agenda of one church. Rather, lasting unity can only be realized through honest and ongoing dialogue among free and committed participants.

The Orthodox churches have articulated their experience of being silenced by the majority within the context of the modern ecumenical movement as well. This concern precipitated conversations around the decision-making procedures in the World Council of Churches in the latter part of the twentieth century. Largely motivated by the perspective of the Orthodox, the shift toward a consensus model of decision making in the WCC provides a context for evaluating the appropriateness of Habermas's discourse theory in ecumenical dialogue. The example of the Council of Florence provides an extreme example of a majority perspective shaping the outcome of dialogue. This is helpful to keep in mind as I apply Habermas's theory to the consensus model of deliberation in chapter 4.

(d) Finally, the Council of Florence also reminds us of the importance of honest representation of one's context. Many factors contributed to the inability of the Orthodox participants to represent their church's teaching at the Council of Florence. In Spivak's terminology, they could not speak in their condition of subalternity at the council. This case reveals the reality of power dynamics at play in ecumenical encounters, which occurs in more subtle ways as well. Using the language of Habermas, the dialogue that occurred on a formal institutional level could not be received as relevant to the Orthodox church because it did not adequately speak to the shared truths of their lifeworld. Spivak's postcolonial insight serves to remind us of the limitations of Habermas's discourse theory, which relies on the possibility of the free exchange of truth claims. It is important to acknowledge the impossibility of achieving this ideal in real-life contexts. At the same time, Habermas's theory of discourse offers one way to move forward in the effort to create dominance-free discourse. Spivak's caution to acknowledge the limitations of our always contextually embedded theories is helpful as we discern Habermas's contribution to ecumenical dialogue. I will revisit the conversation on the role of the institution/system of representation and the role of the ecclesial tradition/lifeworld in chapter 4, when I explore the implications of Habermas's social theory on the question of the nature and purpose of the World Council of Churches.

These principles are not new in the ecumenical movement. The Second Vatican Council's Decree on Ecumenism, *Unitatis Redintegratio*, also expresses these themes. The document stresses the need for dialogue to be built upon mutual respect, as well as the need to make "every effort to avoid expressions, judgments and actions which do not represent the condition of our separated brethren with truth and fairness and so make mutual relations with them more difficult" (UR 4). It goes on to instruct Catholics to participate in ecumenical dialogue without losing sight of their duty to honestly represent the Catholic Church in such dialogues, which involves acknowledging the real divisions that exist (UR 4). Examined alongside the story of the Council of Florence, the Catholic approach to ecumenism laid out in *Unitatis Redintegratio* reveals the development of a modern ecumenical spirit that differs remarkably from earlier attempts to reunite the Christian church.

While these examples from history seem extreme, they are helpful in highlighting what not to do in ecumenical dialogue today. Even though it seems absurd that any church would approach Christian unity with the assumptions or motivations that we see in the *Henoticon* and the Council of Florence, these mistakes are evident in more subtle ways within the contemporary ecumenical movement. Ecumenical efforts today are much more in line with Habermas's theory of discourse. Recent statements between the churches highlight both the common assumptions and the areas of disagreement. This is evident in the recent statement on ecclesiology, which states what the churches have in common and what they do not hold in common.[55] In effect, this method provides an opportunity for the churches to raise truth claims and to freely agree or disagree. One can question the real possibility of freedom in a communicative encounter—this is particularly relevant in the context of the Council of Florence. However, the first step in effective ecumenical dialogue is the willingness to speak one's own truth and hear the truth of the other. This process may reveal conflicting truths, but examining these conflicts is a necessary step in resolving them.

A critical analysis of these historical case studies reveals some important insights into the process of dialogue and the possibility of consensus. While not without limitations, Habermas's theory of communicative action provides one viable framework for ecumenical dialogue. By pointing out some of the ways that dominance-free discourse can be promoted, even if not entirely achieved, Habermas's discourse theory can help the churches relate to each other more effectively. In the following chapters, I will draw upon this theory to engage in pressing questions for contemporary ecumenists, offering a constructive proposal for how to move forward in ecumenical dialogue.

---

[55] See the Faith and Order Commission's *The Nature and Mission of the Church: A Stage on the Way to a Common Statement* (Geneva: WCC, 2005) as an example of this contemporary method.

3

Visions of Unity in the Ecumenical Movement

The formation of the World Council of Churches (WCC) in 1948 not only marks a significant moment in the history of the ecumenical movement but also can be appreciated for its importance on a broader scale of Western history. Along with the formation of the United Nations in 1945, the WCC responded to the growing awareness of the need for global cooperation in the aftermath of two world wars. Within this context, there was an evident need to foster peaceful manifestations of unity in diversity. The World Council of Churches emerged as an avenue for cooperation between the Life and Work Movement and the Faith and Order Movement, both of which formed in 1910 as a way for Christian churches to grow together and foster unity. Though the ecumenical movement did not begin with the World Council of Churches, the gathering in Amsterdam that formed the WCC left a permanent mark on the history of Christianity because the formation of the WCC provided an unprecedented level of organization for the promotion of Christian unity.[1]

From the beginning of the particular trajectory within the ecumenical movement that has been shaped by the WCC, different approaches to unity shaped the identities and activities of participating churches and organizations. Life and Work promoted unity through shared life and service, while Faith and Order promoted unity through dialogue and theological reflection. While these visions are not necessarily opposed, they emphasize different aspects of the ecumenical goal. In other words, they offer different answers to the questions of "Why unity?" and "What kind of unity?" Debates around the nature of the unity we seek in the ecumenical movement have taken shape around a variety of perspectives. The conversation between Life and Work and Faith and Order is just one example of such debates that I will take up in this chapter. This chapter

---

[1] Willem A. Visser 't Hooft, *The Genesis and Formation of the World Council of Churches* (Geneva: WCC Publications, 1982), 58–60.

will also explore conversations between United and Uniting churches and Christian World Communions. These dialogues frame the debate around the nature of visible unity, particularly engaging the question of how much confessional diversity should be maintained in the unity we seek. The debate around the relationship between diversity and communion are still relevant today, emerging in the recent Faith and Order document on ecclesiology, *The Nature and Mission of the Church: A Stage on the Way to a Common Statement.*[2]

Acknowledging the complexity and perhaps anticipating the challenge of defining a common vision of unity, during its formative years the World Council of Churches refrained from making definitive statements on the goal of ecumenism. The council's openness on the question of unity is tied to its recognition of the ecclesiological diversity of the churches that participate in the ecumenical movement. Questions about the nature of unity and the role of the WCC in promoting that unity are essentially ecclesiological. In other words, the understanding of the nature of one's particular church will shape one's understanding of the nature of the larger Christian church, whose unity we seek to manifest in the ecumenical movement. The connection between the vision of the one church of Christ, the self-understandings of the churches that participate in that church, and the nature of the World Council of Churches is laid out in the "Toronto statement" entitled "The Church, the Churches and the World Council of Churches." The Toronto statement has served as a touchstone for conversations around the nature of unity. Drafted in 1950, the insights of the Toronto statement are still relevant for the ecumenical movement today as we continue to wrestle with questions about the nature of unity within the reality of ecclesiological plurality.

In this chapter, I present the shape of the conversations around the nature of unity in the history of the World Council of Churches. My point of entry into this conversation is the Toronto statement, particularly the debates around its development and the role that it has played in ecclesiological dialogues in the ecumenical movement. Using the tools obtained from my critical appreciation of Habermas's thought to analyze these conversations, I argue that the Toronto statement provides an important framework for the question of what unity means. The Toronto statement's insistence that we cannot presuppose the nature of unity allows us to avoid strategic action toward a predetermined goal that may

---

[2] WCC Commission on Faith and Order, *The Nature and Mission of the Church: A Stage on the Way to a Common Statement* (Geneva: WCC, 2005).

not resonate with every participant. Ecclesiological diversity requires ecclesiological openness when we consider the nature of Christian unity. Following this thesis, the objectives of this chapter are to convey the complexity surrounding the development and reception of the Toronto statement; to describe the subsequent debates on unity, highlighting references to the Toronto statement; to give context for the contemporary questions on ecclesiology that inform our understandings of unity; and to offer a constructive proposal for addressing these questions by using the insights of contemporary critical theory.

THE QUESTION OF UNITY IN THE DEVELOPMENT AND RECEPTION OF THE TORONTO STATEMENT

Any discussion about the origins of the World Council of Churches would be incomplete without giving particular attention to the contribution of its first general secretary, Willem A. Visser 't Hooft. We discover his voice behind many of the pivotal texts in the formation of the WCC. Visser 't Hooft was particularly vocal in supporting the drafting of the Toronto statement and encouraging the WCC to remain faithful to its insights about the nature of unity within the reality of ecclesiological pluralism. An analysis of his vision of the WCC as expressed in his participation in drafting the Toronto statement and his defense of the Toronto statement against critiques reveals his strong commitment to the inclusivity of the World Council of Churches. He saw the Toronto statement as one way to ensure ecclesial and cultural inclusivity. He stated:

> Real ecumenism presupposes a respect for the beliefs of the partners with whom one enters into dialogue, treating them not as an ideological smokescreen but as real convictions. Clearly, non-theological factors play an important role in the churches' ecumenical policy, and institutional self-assertion is one of the strongest of these factors. We must however not become so obsessed with them that we neglect the very real theological convictions which also influence that policy. The World Council is the forum where those holding these convictions enter into conversation, and where no church need fear that it will be put under pressure to change its position—except the pressure that may be exercised by new truth discovered in the ecumenical encounter. The originality and the *raison d'être* of the World Council lie precisely in this respect for differences.[3]

---

[3] Visser 't Hooft, *The Genesis of the World Council of Churches*, 84–85.

Anticipating the development of the Toronto statement, Visser 't Hooft discerned the need for a statement in response to growing misconceptions about the World Council of Churches on the nature of the council and what membership in the council meant. The basis of the WCC was articulated at the First General Assembly in Amsterdam. [4] While the basis of the WCC lays out the foundational premises of its member churches, it does not say much about the nature of the council or the vision of Christian unity that it promotes. In preparation for the First General Assembly of the WCC in Amsterdam, Visser 't Hooft addressed some misconceptions about the burgeoning council in his paper "The World Council of Churches: Its Nature—Its Limits."[5] In this paper he noted the significance of the WCC, distinguishing it from other ecumenical organizations such as Life and Work and Faith and Order. Since the WCC is a permanent ecumenical body that aims to be more inclusive in terms of its membership and influence, he argued that there needed to be careful discussion about the nature of membership and the purpose of the council.[6]

Visser 't Hooft's preparatory document voiced a number of the considerations laid out in the Toronto statement. Many of the concerns that he addresses pertain to the nature of the WCC, its relationship to the one church of Christ, and its authority to speak on behalf of the churches. I will take up the conversation around the WCC's authority to speak in the next chapter. The other set of concerns relate directly to the question at hand; namely, how can the WCC talk about the nature of unity in such a way that respects the diverse ecclesiologies of member churches and nonmember churches. Visser 't Hooft stressed the need for the WCC

---

[4] The basis of the World Council of Churches, drafted at the First General Assembly at Amsterdam, states that "The World Council of Churches is a fellowship of churches which accept our Lord Jesus Christ as God and Savior." First General Assembly at Amsterdam, "The Constitution of the World Council of Churches," in Willem A. Visser 't Hooft, ed., *The First Assembly of the World Council of Churches* (New York: Harper and Brothers, 1949), 197. This underwent minor revisions at the New Delhi Assembly and at the Harare Assembly, but it served to articulate the basic nature of the WCC during its formative years.

[5] Willem A. Visser 't Hooft, "The World Council of Churches: Its Nature—Its Limits," (First Draft) Study 47E/102A, March 1947 (Geneva: World Council of Churches Study Dept., 1947).

[6] Willem A. Visser 't Hooft, "The Significance of the World Council of Churches," in World Council of Churches, *The Universal Church in God's Design* (London: SCM Press, 1948), 177.

to remain open on the question of the nature of the church in order to facilitate inclusive participation in the council. Openness, he explained, means that "the council by its nature does not assume one conception of the church."[7]

Visser 't Hooft's position was largely motivated by concern for the Orthodox churches. He wanted the WCC to ensure that the Orthodox could be members in the council without compromising their ecclesial self-understandings and commitments.[8] For example, Orthodox ecclesiology complicates the idea of "mutual recognition"—acknowledging the ecclesial status of other churches. One can observe a consideration of the Orthodox position in the Toronto statement, which asserts that mutual recognition is not a prerequisite for membership in the WCC. During the drafting of the Toronto statement, there was significant debate around the topic of mutual recognition among churches, highlighting the potential divisiveness of different ecclesiologies.[9] Some participants articulated the need for churches to recognize the full ecclesial status of other churches. Others noted that full mutual recognition would be impossible for churches whose ecclesiologies prohibited them from acknowledging the fullness of church outside of their own church. This view was expressed by Orthodox participant Fr. Florovsky, who addressed the issue of mutual recognition by saying, "Some members regard other Churches as *essentially* incomplete. If it is felt undesirable or impossible to retain such members, and hence such cleavages in the WCC, it had better be said clearly and plainly."[10] Florovsky's point speaks to the purpose of the Toronto statement. The Toronto statement was the WCC's answer to the question of what membership in the council meant, and within this context the desire for inclusive membership guided the statement on the nature of the council.

In addition to the ecclesiological concerns, Visser 't Hooft explicitly wanted to make sure that the WCC did not follow an exclusively Western worldview, and he did this by encouraging relationships with the

---

[7] Visser 't Hooft, "The World Council of Churches: Its Nature—Its Limits," 28.

[8] Report by the General Secretary, in *Minutes and Reports of the Meeting of the Provisional Committee of the World Council of Churches, Buck Hill Falls, Penn., April 1947* (Geneva: WCC, 1947), 54.

[9] See responses to the Toronto statement in the *The Ecumenical Review* 3, no. 3 (April 1951): 213–57.

[10] *Minutes and Reports of the Third Meeting of the Central Committee of the World Council of Churches Toronto, July 9–15, 1950* (Geneva: WCC, 1950), 16.

Orthodox churches. The Orthodox presence in the council offered a non-Western theological and cultural perspective in the WCC, which was composed primarily of mainstream Protestant traditions. It is important to note that concerns about inclusivity and diversity were present from the beginning of the World Council of Churches. One can observe these issues in later discussions surrounding decision-making procedures in the WCC, where the Orthodox churches advocated for a consensus model of deliberation to avoid the marginalization of underrepresented churches. For this reason, I suggest that insights gleaned from these earlier conversations around unity in diversity can be retrieved to inform contemporary debates.

Stressing that the World Council of Churches' existence and authority is derivative from the member churches, the Toronto statement declares that the WCC is not a "superchurch." The implications of the ecclesial neutrality of the WCC will be discussed in the next chapter. What is important in this context is the fact that the WCC does not itself claim to have a specific ecclesial self-understanding, because it does not understand itself to be a superchurch. Consequently, the WCC is not guided by a particular ecclesiology, nor can it claim a preunderstanding of what the one church of Christ will look like. In the words of the Toronto statement, "It does not prejudge the ecclesiological problem."[11] On the one hand, the declaration of the neutrality of the WCC with respect to the nature of unity opens the council to the possibility of more diverse membership. On the other hand, it does not clearly delineate the goal of the ecumenical movement, leaving some participants wanting more definition of the unity we seek.

The Toronto statement had a mixed reception, as evidenced in the documented responses to the text.[12] Some respondents to the document affirmed the value of ecclesiological neutrality at that point in the life of the council. They argued that the current position of the WCC on the unity question did not eliminate the possibility of coming to a clearer vision of unity in the future. Some proponents of this perspective suggested that the Faith and Order Commission make ecclesiology a top priority for further study so that the churches could come to a common under-

[11] WCC Central Committee at Toronto, "The Church, the Churches and the World Council of Churches: The Ecclesiological Significance of the World Council of Churches," in Lukas Vischer, ed., *A Documentary History of the Faith and Order Movement 1927–1963* (St. Louis, MO: Bethany Press, 1963), 170.

[12] See responses to the Toronto statement in *The Ecumenical Review* 3, no. 3 (April 1951): 213–57.

standing of unity. Others noted that the basis of the WCC provided a significant acknowledgement of the unity that was already present despite ecclesiological differences. They argued that the churches did not need to have doctrinal consensus on the nature of the church and the nature of unity if they remembered their commonality expressed in the basis of the WCC, which locates unity in a common faith and baptism.[13]

One of the most vocal objectors to some of the principles in the Toronto statement was Bishop Newbigin. Fearing that too much neutrality would lead to complacency, Newbigin cautioned the churches against becoming too comfortable with a lack of consensus on the nature of the church. With regard to the authority and longevity of the Toronto statement he states, "The more permanent it becomes, the more will it tend to become, in effect, committed to a certain kind of answer to that question. And it will be the wrong answer, because the proper embodiment of that idea is the Church and not a Council of Churches."[14] From Newbigin's perspective the Toronto statement "defines the starting-point, and not the way or the goal."[15] His position invites the churches to dialogue on ecclesiology so that the council could move from neutrality to commonality. Newbigin had a lot to say on the nature of the WCC, which we will explore in the next chapter. However, it is worth noting here that Newbigin and others who shared his perspective were wary of the WCC becoming a neutral organization of churches instead of a manifestation of the unified church that they were seeking.

In the years following the promulgation of the Toronto statement, debates ensued around the longevity of the text in the life of the council. Did the council intend for the Toronto statement to have a timeless status in the WCC? Could the council outgrow the need for neutrality on the question of ecclesiology? The debates around the reception of the document laid the foundation for further discussion around the need to preserve the Toronto statement. Newbigin's caution against getting stuck in neutrality was voiced by those who argued that the council was moving toward a greater understanding of the unity we seek and could therefore make a more definitive unity statement. Visser 't Hooft led the defense of

---

[13] For example, see Clarence Craig, "The Reality of the Church and Our Doctrines about the Church," and the bishop of Malmesbury, "Can We Stay Together?" *The Ecumenical Review* 3, no. 3 (April 1951): 231–37.

[14] Bishop Newbigin, "Comments on 'The Church, the Churches and the World Council of Churches,'" *The Ecumenical Review* 3, no. 3 (April 1951): 253.

[15] Ibid., 253.

the Toronto statement, arguing that openness to the unity question was still necessary in light of ecclesiological differences that were becoming even more apparent.[16]

This debate framed conversations around the preparation for the Third General Assembly of the WCC in New Delhi (1963). The Faith and Order Commission asserted its role in promoting the visible unity of the churches by stating more clearly the nature of the unity that we seek. This involved a move away from the position of neutrality that was expressed in the Toronto statement, although it would not be accurate to say that there was a firm rejection of the text.[17] Multiple factors motivated this action by the Faith and Order Commission. It is important to explore these factors because the statement of unity at New Delhi became a touchstone for subsequent discussions on unity.[18]

One of the motivating factors behind Faith and Order's efforts to define more explicitly the WCC's vision of unity was the concern that there was a growing impatience for Christian unity experienced among young people. The Faith and Order Commission of the Fourth General Assembly at Uppsala reported that "many contemporary youth, preoccupied with Christian witness and action in our world, are dissatisfied with the slow progress made by the churches toward the unity they have so often proclaimed."[19] Coupled with an impatience for the approach of the WCC in promoting Christian unity was a developing apathy toward the ecumenical movement in general. Within the context of multiple social revolutions of the 1960s, many young people questioned the importance of promoting Christian unity when the demands of the world took priority for attention and action. The Faith and Order Commission wanted to make a case for ecumenical dialogue to a skeptical audience of young social activists.[20]

---

[16] Willem A. Visser 't Hooft, "Various Meanings of Unity and the Unity Which the World Council of Churches Seeks to Promote," in *The Ecumenical Review* 8, no. 1 (October 1955): 18–29.

[17] *Workbook for the Assembly Committees*, Prepared for the Third Assembly of the World Council of Churches, New Delhi, 1961 (Geneva: WCC, 1961), 78–79.

[18] See Melanie May, "The Unity We Share and the Unity we Seek," in Briggs et al., *The History of the Ecumenical Movement*, vol. 3, 84–86, and Harding Meyer, *That All May Be One: Perceptions and Models of Ecumenicity*, trans. William Rusch (Grand Rapids, MI: Eerdmans, 1999), 43.

[19] Norman Goodall, ed., *The Uppsala Report: Official Report of the Fourth Assembly of the World Council of Churches Uppsala July 4–20, 1968* (Geneva: WCC, 1968), 223.

[20] *Workbook for the Assembly Committees*, Prepared for the Third Assembly of the World Council of Churches, New Delhi, 1961 (Geneva: WCC, 1961), 78–79.

All of these factors considered, perhaps the primary reason behind the development of the New Delhi unity statement was the belief among the majority of the council that the WCC had grown in understanding of what unity meant and that they could therefore articulate it more accurately than was possible in 1950.[21] The Central Committee meeting at St. Andrews (1960) focused on the question of how to move forward on pronouncing a clearer definition of unity. The meeting minutes indicate some trepidation about making definitive statements about unity, while at the same time identifying the imperative to move forward. Interestingly, they cite the Toronto statement in support of this endeavor, saying that "difficult as it may be to move forward in this treacherous area of dogmatic agreement on unity, to stand still would be finally to deny the affirmation of the Toronto Statement that 'the Council exists to break the deadlock between the churches.'"[22]

The unity statement drafted at the Third General Assembly of the World Council of Churches in New Delhi is more explicit about the nature of the church's unity than previous statements. It reads:

> We believe that the unity which is both God's will and his gift to his Church is being made visible as all in each place who are baptized into Jesus Christ and confess him as Lord and Savior are brought by the Holy Spirit into one fully committed fellowship, holding the one apostolic faith, preaching one Gospel, breaking one bread, joining in common prayer, and having a corporate life reaching out in witness and service to all and who at the same time are united with the whole Christian fellowship in all places and all ages in such wise that ministry and members are accepted by all, and that all can act and speak together as occasion requires for the tasks to which God calls his people.[23]

There is a specificity with which the assembly articulates the WCC's vision of unity in the New Delhi statement. The understanding of unity indicated in this statement makes explicit demands on the churches in order to manifest Christian unity in each locality. If unity is going to be made visible "all in each place," it "will involve nothing less than a death

[21] Ibid., 78–79.

[22] WCC Central Committee Meeting at St. Andrews, "St. Andrews Central Committee Meeting Minutes," World Council of Churches Archives (box 23.2.003), 43.

[23] Third General Assembly of the World Council of Churches at New Delhi, "Report of the Section on Unity," in Lukas Vischer, ed., A *Documentary History*, 144–45.

and rebirth for many forms of church life as we have known them."[24]
While this definition of unity can find its expression in different models
of unity, it is particularly conducive to the model of organic unity.[25] The
history of the WCC reveals the difficulty of ascribing to a particular
model of unity because of the diverse ecclesiologies of the WCC's member churches. Debates surrounding the nature of unity complicate Faith
and Order's task. While the New Delhi unity statement is undeniably
an important achievement in the history of the WCC, it did not resolve
ecclesiological debates about unity, nor did it make the Toronto statement obsolete. This is evident in the subsequent debates on the nature
of unity, particularly the debate on whether unity should be understood
as an organic unity or as a unity in diversity.

The unity statement of New Delhi raised the question, for some ecumenists, of the relevance of the Toronto statement. Some saw the move
toward a more explicit definition of unity as a way of moving beyond the
Toronto statement, making its neutral position outdated in the WCC.
Ernest Payne articulated this perspective, suggesting,

> The importance of the Third Assembly's report becomes even more
> apparent if it is compared with the widely quoted Toronto State-
> ment. . . . The Toronto Statement deals primarily, of course, with
> the World Council of Churches itself and will require renewed exami-
> nation in the light of the concluding part of the report of the Third
> Assembly's section on Unity.[26]

Visser 't Hooft, cautioned against precipitously abandoning the Toronto statement, arguing that the principles of ecclesiological neutrality
and openness to different approaches to unity were still necessary char-
acteristics of the WCC. In his publication on the formative years of the
World Council of Churches, Visser 't Hooft identified the period of time
around the New Delhi assembly when there was an effort to go beyond

---

[24] *Workbook for the Assembly Committees*, Prepared for the Third Assembly of the World
Council of Churches, New Delhi, 1961 (Geneva: WCC, 1961), 78.

[25] See Melanie May, who associates the model of organic union with the New Delhi
statement on unity involving "nothing less than a death or rebirth of many forms of church
life as we have known them." New Delhi report as quoted in May, "The Unity We Have
and the Unity We Seek," in Briggs et al., *History of the Ecumenical Movement*, vol. 3, 96.
I am using the term "organic union" in the same way, emphasizing the high demands
for immediate and localized unity, which necessitates a loss of confessional difference.

[26] Ernest Payne, "Working Out the New Delhi Statement on Unity," *The Ecumenical
Review* 14, no. 3 (April 1962): 297.

the Toronto statement on the question of unity. This led to an attempt by the Faith and Order Commission at Montreal (1965) to revise the Toronto statement. In response to this, Visser 't Hooft suggested that the council was not ready to reformulate the Toronto statement, even though it was good to discuss its relevance in light of developments on the unity question. Reinforcing his position, Visser 't Hooft quoted Professor Berkhof, saying, "We can live beyond Toronto, but we cannot formulate beyond Toronto."[27]

Debates around the relevance of the Toronto statement will resurface throughout the history of the council. This formative period of the WCC (1948–61) reveals prototypical perspectives within these debates. Those who emphasize the need for the WCC to maintain neutrality on the nature of unity lift up the Toronto statement as a classic document in the WCC's self-understanding. Those who emphasize the need to move forward on the unity question highlight the time-bound quality of the Toronto statement and challenge the perpetual neutrality of the WCC's perspective on unity.

These debates raise questions about the nature of discourse and the possibility of reaching understanding across difference. Habermas's discourse theory, which offers a model for achieving commonality within a pluralistic context, is particularly helpful in addressing this ecumenical debate. From this framework, Visser 't Hooft is correct in his insistence upon openness on the nature of unity for the sake of creating inclusivity within the WCC. Inclusivity is one of the prerequisites for achieving consensus through discourse. If a discourse is going to be complete, it must invite all voices affected by the outcome to be heard. Holding back from making explicit ecclesiological commitments is necessary for creating the kind of dominance-free discourse that Habermas imagines as key for rational agreement. Visser 't Hooft's concern for creating pathways for non-Western/non-Protestant views is particularly remarkable for that period in history. He recognized the ways in which voices can be excluded by the dominant agenda, and he made an explicit effort to create a space for diverse traditions in the WCC.

The history of the WCC reveals that no single vision of unity works for all churches because one's perspective on the nature of unity is shaped by one's ecclesiology. The next section of this chapter will map out some of the debates around the nature of visible unity that emerged after

---

[27] Visser 't Hooft, *The Genesis and Formation of the World Council of Churches*, 83.

New Delhi. The diversity of perspectives on unity complicates the task of organizing these debates. However, in order to grasp the significance of the debates, which I argue make the case for the relevance of the Toronto statement today, it is important to understand the trajectory of the conversation. For the purposes of highlighting the complexity of the unity question, I will focus on the debates between the Faith and Order Commission and the Life and Work Commission on approaches to Christian unity. I will then highlight debates between the United and Uniting churches and Christian World Communions on models of Christian unity.

TWENTIETH-CENTURY DEBATES ON UNITY

The development and the reception of the New Delhi unity statement raised questions about the timeless applicability of the Toronto statement. Was it necessary for the WCC to remain neutral on the unity question indefinitely? Were they ready to make a pronouncement on the nature of unity that could resonate with diverse ecclesiologies? Did the New Delhi statement on unity make the Toronto statement obsolete? These questions are particularly relevant for the WCC but have broader implications in the ecumenical movement. Some ecumenists argued that the New Delhi statement went too far in defining unity, pointing out the potential divisiveness of having a preferred model of unity in the WCC.[28] This objection turned out to be relevant in the years to come, when some churches challenged the universal appropriateness of the organic model of unity.[29]

The vision of unity promoted at New Delhi most directly supports the model of organic union. This is evident in the emphasis on local expressions of commonality that necessitate a transformation of confessional identity and practice. Recall that the assembly texts suggest that the demands of unity require a death and rebirth of the churches as we know them. Melanie May aligns this position with the model of organic union. She suggests that the general assembly at New Delhi promoted

---

[28] See responses to the New Delhi report, particularly Prof. Norgaard of Denmark who suggested that "the description on unity went too far. The quest for uniformity will always create division." in Willem A. Visser 't Hooft, ed., *The New Delhi Report: The Third Assembly of the World Council of Churches 1961* (London: SCM Press, 1962), 135.

[29] I am using the term "organic union" to mean the approach to unity that emphasizes visible and local communion that necessitates a loss of confessional diversity. I am following Melanie May on this understanding. See her discussion of organic union in Melanie May, "The Unity We Have and the Unity We Seek," in Briggs et al., eds., *The History of the Ecumenical Movement*, vol. 3, 96.

the model of organic union as a preferred model for the WCC.[30] Accepting her thesis, I argue that the move toward a preferred model of unity is problematic because it contradicts the Toronto statement. This argument is grounded in my conviction that the Toronto statement provides a necessary foundation for inclusive dialogue in light of ecclesiological diversity. Again, if we presuppose the nature of unity, we risk excluding voices that do not support that vision.

The New Delhi statement proved to be more prominent within conversations on unity in the twentieth century than the Toronto statement. Harding Meyer supports this claim, arguing that the New Delhi statement was "a decisive step, which cannot be estimated highly enough for the development of the ecumenical movement. . . . All later declarations on unity, both within and outside the World Council, stand, so to speak, on the shoulders of this first declaration on unity."[31] One can observe references to New Delhi in subsequent assembly statements on unity, as well as in Faith and Order works throughout the century.[32] The New Delhi statement served as a touchstone for further developments on the unity question. This could explain the predominance of the model of organic union in the WCC until the 1970s.[33] I agree with Meyer that the privileged position of the New Delhi statement on unity gives preference to the model of organic unity in twentieth-century conversations on unity. I also suggest that this is contradictory to the Toronto statement's affirmation that "membership in the World Council does not imply the acceptance of a specific doctrine concerning the nature of Church unity."[34] This assumption underlies my argument for a Habermasian approach to ecumenical dialogue, which provides a theoretical support for the ecclesiological neutrality expressed in the Toronto statement.

The privileged status of the New Delhi statement on unity had implications for Faith and Order's post–New Delhi work on unity. Faith and

---

[30] Ibid., 96.

[31] Meyer, *That All May Be One*, 43.

[32] The report of the general assembly in Nairobi on what unity requires refers to the New Delhi statement, stating, "As the New Delhi Assembly pointed out, they [Christian churches] are bound together because they have received the same baptism and share the same Eucharist." The Fifth Assembly in Nairobi, "Nairobi 1975: Section II On What Unity Requires," in Günther Gassmann, ed., *A Documentary History of Faith and Order: 1963–1993* (Geneva: WCC, 1993), 3.

[33] Meyer, *That All May Be One*, 100.

[34] WCC Central Committee at Toronto, "The Church, Churches and the World Council of Churches," in Vischer, *A Documentary History*, 171.

Order explored multiple dimensions of unity but returned to the New Delhi statement as a touchstone. The Fifth General Assembly in Nairobi (1975) lifted up conciliarity as a feature of the unity we seek. In doing so, they built upon the theme of catholicity that had been highlighted by the Fourth General Assembly in Uppsala (1968). Conciliarity is a visible embodiment of catholicity, providing a tangible and functional manifestation of the universality of the Christian church. Faith and Order continued to explore the implications of conciliarity on the ecumenical movement at their 1973 meeting in Salamanca. The report issued from Salamanca describes the nature of conciliarity as a "fellowship of churches that are truly united."[35] The text goes on to stress that conciliar fellowship presupposes organic union. Conciliar fellowship is not presented as an alternative to organic union and therefore is not intended to replace the New Delhi statement on unity. Harding Meyer questions Salamanca's decision to tie conciliarity to organic union, suggesting that there can be expressions of conciliarity that do not presuppose organic union.[36] In actuality, while the WCC may have been privileging the model of organic union, there were other approaches to unity that had emerged in the post–New Delhi period of the ecumenical movement.

Meyer points out that alternative models to organic union surfaced during the 1970s,[37] challenging the notion that the member churches of the WCC had come to a firm consensus on what unity meant and what model could best serve the ecumenical movement. The conversations on unity in that period revealed the need for the WCC to remain open to diverse perspectives on the nature of unity if they were to maintain their commitment to the inclusive vision of membership promoted by the Toronto statement. A greater attention to ecclesiology in the years after New Delhi showed that some of the ecclesiological presuppositions of the model of organic union were not shared by all participants in the WCC.[38]

---

[35] "The Unity of the Church—the Next Steps: Report of the Salamanca Consultation Convened by the Faith and Order Commission, WCC on 'Concepts of Unity and Models of Union' Sept. 1973," in WCC Commission on Faith and Order, *What Kind of Unity?* (Geneva: WCC, 1974).

[36] Meyer, *That All May Be One,* 122.

[37] In his study, Meyer illustrates confessional differences behind understandings of unity. His work ties organic union to a particular ecclesiology, challenging the view that it is the most inclusive, accessible, or appropriate model for the WCC to adopt. See Meyer, *That All May Be One.*

[38] This became particularly evident after *Baptism, Eucharist and Ministry* (1982) highlighted ecclesiology as a major area of disagreement in ecumenical dialogue.

The model of organic union works well for churches that emphasize local expressions of unity. Among the primary supporters of this model are those churches that identify with United and Uniting churches, such as the United Church of Christ. Paul Crow explains that United and Uniting churches emphasize local unity through consensus and commitment. While they recognize that cultural and confessional identities are important, they also testify to the belief that confessional identities are provisional in the life of the churches.[39] United and Uniting churches have cautioned against any tendencies to emphasize confessional identity within the ecumenical movement. In 1983 Michael Kinnamon referred to discussion among United and Uniting churches about the dangers of new confessionalism threatening the potential of the churches to achieve organic union.[40]

Understandably, United and Uniting churches and Christian World Communions have experienced tension on many issues within the ecumenical movement. World Confessional Communions, such as the Lutheran World Federation, create global interconnections between churches in the same tradition, allowing them to participate in bilateral and multilateral dialogues with a larger confessional presence. United and Uniting churches and Christian World Communions operate on different perspectives on how to structure representation of the churches in ecumenical organizations. United and Uniting churches tend to promote regional representation in the WCC and in national councils, while Christian World Communions foster bilateral and multilateral dialogues through confessional representation.

In response to the accusation that Christian World Communions hinder the churches' progress toward full, visible unity, Harding Meyer points out that their ecumenical commitment often includes a commitment to fostering local unity.[41] Furthermore, he suggests that Christian World Communions serve the ecumenical movement by reminding the churches that unity does not mean uniformity. They stress that confessional and contextual differences are not necessarily divisive.[42] Christian

---

[39] Paul Crow, "United and Uniting Churches: Perspectives from the Colombo Consultation," in Thomas Best and Michael Kinnamon, eds., *Called to Be One in Christ: United Churches and the Ecumenical Movement* (Geneva: WCC, 1985), 5.

[40] Michael Kinnamon, "United Churches and the Christian World Communions," in Best and Kinnamon, eds., *Called to Be One in Christ*, 14.

[41] Harding Meyer, "Christian World Communions: Identity and Ecumenical Calling," *The Ecumenical Review* 46, no. 4 (October 1994): 383–93.

[42] Ibid., 383–93.

World Communions have presented alternative models of unity that reflect their commitment to honoring contextual and confessional diversity.

One such model emerged out of Lutheran–Roman Catholic dialogues on the nature of unity. In the document "Facing Unity" they identify several models of unity that have emerged out of the ecumenical movement, including organic union and conciliar fellowship, raising the question of whether the latter requires the former model. Based on their dialogue, they articulated a preference for the model of "unity in reconciled diversity." This model acknowledges the room for differences that are no longer divisive. It requires commitment to the process of reconciliation, but it does not require an abandonment of one's confessional identity. They emphasize that this model should not be seen as a complacent promoter of mere coexistence. Rather, unity in reconciled diversity promotes true fellowship.[43]

Disagreements around the nature of unity did not form solely around the evaluation of models. One can observe another debate on unity that has been, in many ways, a continuous thread that has taken on different forms. This debate pertains to the question of "Why unity?"—for the church or for the world. Where should we locate the focus of ecumenical activity—in fostering consensus or in engaging in common mission? It seems unfitting to make sharp distinctions between these objectives since there is a general consensus in the WCC that both actions are necessary. At the same time, it is helpful to examine these distinctions because they have historically tended to shape different approaches to unity.

The World Council of Churches formed as a collaborative effort between two ecumenical organizations: the Faith and Order Movement and the Life and Work Movement. While these movements share a commitment to Christian unity, they exemplify two distinct and complimentary approaches to ecumenism. Faith and Order promotes visible unity through their efforts to identify and foster doctrinal consensus among the churches. Life and Work promotes Christian unity in the form of common witness and cooperative response to the needs of the world. Again, the World Council of Churches is itself a testimony to the importance of both approaches to Christian unity. However, tensions have arisen in the ecumenical movement from the privileging of one approach over the other.

The ecumenical dictum "service unites—doctrine divides" speaks to the perspective that privileges the focus of Life and Work over Faith

---

[43] "Facing Unity: Models, Forms, and Phases of Catholic-Lutheran Church Fellowship," in Rusch and Gros, eds., *Deepening Communion: International Ecumenical Documents with Roman Catholic Participation* (Washington, DC: USCCB, 1998), 15–24.

and Order. Proponents of this idea stress the importance of the churches cooperating in response to the world. Christian service unites churches across theological differences, while dialogue on doctrinal issues highlights what divides them. Visser 't Hooft framed this ongoing debate by raising the question of whether the ecumenical movement should be organized around the agenda of the world or the agenda of the churches. This tension, he suggests, has always been present in the ecumenical movement, and there has always been a need for both concerns.[44]

The connection between church unity and social concerns was taken up explicitly by Faith and Order in the study *Church and World: The Unity of the Church and the Renewal of the Human Community*. Conducted from 1982 to 1989, this study coincided with an increased attention to ecclesiology in the Faith and Order Commission after the publication of *Baptism, Eucharist and Ministry* (BEM) in 1982. The *Unity and Renewal* study drew upon an ecclesiological concept to unite concern for church unity and concern for the world. Presenting the church as a prophetic sign of the kingdom of God, it connected the nature and mission of the church and articulated the inseparability of concern for the church and concern for the world.[45]

The 1970s and 80s saw the attention to social issues made more explicit within the World Council of Churches. Concern for the needs of the world has always been present in the ecumenical movement. However, the question of whether the WCC could or should speak on behalf of the churches on social matters became a significant debate during this time. One of the loudest voices of concern came from the Orthodox, who identified the WCC's emphasis on social issues as secular ecumenism. They advocated for a return to traditional ecumenism, which followed the Faith and Order Commission's original raison d'être, namely, to foster theological dialogues in order to overcome divisions. In his response to the *Unity and Renewal* study, John Meyendorff suggested that Faith and Order focus on ecclesiology rather than anthropology because the shift toward concern for the renewal of humankind has not made significant strides toward Christian unity and ecclesiological issues are still among the most divisive.[46]

---

[44] Willem A. Visser 't Hooft, *Has the Ecumenical Movement a Future?* (Atlanta: John Knox Press, 1974), 76–97.

[45] See the Faith and Order study document *Church and World: The Unity of the Church and the Renewal of the Human Community* (Geneva: WCC, 1990).

[46] John Meyendorff, "Unity of the Church—Unity of Mankind," *The Ecumenical Review* 24, no.1 (January 1972): 30–33.

The fear that theological issues were more divisive than social issues was challenged by the Faith and Order study *Unity, Renewal and the Community of Women and Men*. This study highlighted internal divisions that the churches experienced with regard to social issues, particularly on the conflicts churches were experiencing due to different perspectives on the role of women in the church. This study followed the publication "Unity in Tension" (1974), which challenged the churches to manifest unity despite the internal conflicts on social issues.[47] As the WCC began talking more explicitly about social issues, the divisiveness of justice-related questions was made apparent.

A clear example of this tension can be observed in debates around the role of women in the church and perspectives on feminism. The *Community of Women and Men* study highlighted conflicts that the churches experienced with regard to gender relations in the church and in the world. Again, the Orthodox churches were vocal in these discussions and continually called Faith and Order back to a focus on doctrine instead of social issues. From the perspective of Orthodox theological anthropology, women and men have different but complimentary roles in the church. They argue that social movements, such as feminism, cannot change a timeless theological truth. As many Protestant churches moved toward the practice of ordaining women, the Orthodox churches feared that redefining women's roles in the church according to secular demands would hinder the progress toward Christian unity.[48]

The debates surrounding the nature and purpose of unity reveal the need for further dialogue on what unity means and why it should be a priority. A comprehensive understanding of unity must address theological conflicts as well as divisions on how to respond to the world. The discussions around the *Unity and Renewal* study highlighted the need for more attention to ecclesiology, as different understandings of the relationship between the church and the world shaped different responses to the study. Furthermore, the debates around models of unity surfaced many implicit disagreements on the nature of the church. Finally, the drafting and reception of Faith and Order's groundbreaking text *Baptism, Eucharist and Ministry* (1982) brought many ecclesiological issues to light and made studies on ecclesiology a top priority for the WCC.

---

[47] Thomas Best, ed., *Beyond Unity-in-Tension: Unity, Renewal and the Community of Women and Men*, Faith and Order paper no. 138 (Geneva: WCC, 1988).

[48] See George Dragas, "Some General Reactions and Comments from an Orthodox Point of View," in Best, ed., *Beyond Unity in Tension*, 117–26.

The period between the publication of *Baptism, Eucharist and Ministry* and *The Nature and Mission of the Church: A Stage on the Way to a Common Statement* (2005) reveals the complexity of ecclesiology in ecumenical dialogues. Discussions on the nature of the church and its relationship to the world reveal a great deal of commonality. At the same time, they highlight some divisive issues that directly impact the way that the churches talk about the nature of unity. The next section of this chapter will explore these conversations, emphasizing the complicated task of articulating a common vision of unity among churches with diverse ecclesiologies. The reality of ecclesiological pluralism, which I illustrate in the next section, invites a retrieval of the principles laid out in the Toronto statement that may guide a constructive proposal on how to move forward on the unity question. My constructive proposal draws upon the insights of Habermas's theory of communicative action, which stresses the importance of achieving common convictions before assuming a common goal. In this case, Habermas reminds us to achieve a common ecclesiological framework before assuming a particular model of unity.

ECCLESIOLOGY SINCE BEM

Baptism, Eucharist and Ministry (BEM), described as the "Lima text" because it was drafted at the 1982 Faith and Order Commission meeting in Lima, Peru, is widely regarded as one of the most significant ecumenical texts in history. This recognition comes from the fact that it comprehensively addresses three fundamental areas of Christian belief and practice: baptism, Eucharist, and ministry. Although the text was drafted by the Faith and Order Commission, the authors note in the preface that the statement is a result of wider efforts.[49] BEM emerges from a variety of bilateral and multilateral dialogues among the churches themselves. In other words, it was born out of a long process of coming to a greater recognition of both the commonalities and the differences in the churches' approaches to these key areas of the Christian faith.

Furthermore, the significance of BEM lies in its reception. Numerous Christian churches took up the task of issuing official responses to BEM, indicating both acceptance and disagreement. Regardless of the mixed feedback, the fact that so many churches responded to the text gives it a

---

[49] WCC Commission on Faith and Order, *Baptism, Eucharist and Ministry* (Geneva: WCC, 1982), preface.

prominent place in the history of the ecumenical movement. An examination of the responses provides a strong indication of the need for more studies and ecumenical dialogues on ecclesiology. Many of the areas of disagreement relate directly or indirectly to questions around the nature and mission of the church. The Faith and Order Commission followed BEM with a focus on ecclesiology, which resulted in three important texts: *On the Way to Fuller Koinonia* (1993), *The Nature and Mission of the Church* (2005), and the Porto Alegre ecclesiology text, "Called to Be the One Church" (2006). I will examine each of these texts in this section; however, in order to appreciate the significance of the texts themselves, one must consider the questions to which they were responding. Hence, I will now explore the ecclesiological concerns that emerged out of the drafting process and the reception of *Baptism, Eucharist and Ministry*.

While the majority of responding churches supported Faith and Order's approach to BEM, some churches raised oppositions to its promulgation. The Greek Orthodox Church refused to issue a formal response to the document because they claimed that BEM exemplified a trend in the WCC that betrayed its foundational vision. They suggested that BEM was released to the churches for a response without involving everyone in the consultative process of its construction. They found this approach to be unacceptable, stressing that common statements must grow organically out of dialogue among the churches. Consensus on doctrinal issues, the Greek Orthodox Church argued, cannot be presupposed by Faith and Order and secondarily confirmed by the churches themselves.[50]

Other methodological objections to BEM relate implicitly to the question of what visible unity means. For churches that do not regard doctrinal consensus as central to visible unity, BEM lacked essential relevance. Many Free Churches objected to BEM's focus on doctrine and ecclesial order because, from their perspective, unity is fundamentally invisible. The Quaker Church of the Netherlands referred to this concern in their official response to BEM by explaining that they experience church unity without dogma and sacraments. Lengthy deliberation on the nature of the sacraments and ecclesial order does not resonate with their ecumenical vision.[51] Several churches echoed this perspective by emphasizing the centrality of faith and/or mission over teaching and order. The Salvation Army opposed to BEM's lack of focus on service as a source

---

[50] A letter from the metropolitan of Peristerion, in Max Thurian, ed., *Churches Respond to BEM*, vol. 5 (Geneva: WCC, 1986), 1–3.

[51] Quakers of the Netherlands, in Thurian, ed., *Churches Respond to BEM*, vol. 3, 297–99.

and expression of Christian unity. Like the Quakers, they regard the church as essentially invisible and consequently do not resonate with the emphasis on visible structures and expressions of the Christian church.[52]

Some respondents to BEM criticized Faith and Order for catering to "high church" ecclesiology in their overemphasis on visible structures and the suggestion that all churches should consider adopting the historical threefold model of ministry. Specifically, the Reformed Church of Scotland suggested that BEM reflects a bias toward Catholic, Orthodox, and Anglican ecclesiology by demanding more compromise from nonepiscopal churches than from episcopal churches.[53] Interestingly, Catholic and Orthodox respondents critiqued the document for lacking a solid ecclesiology and invited Faith and Order to follow up the text with more extensive studies on the nature and mission of the church.[54] Specifically, the Roman Catholic Church applauded BEM for its promotion of unity in common faith, sacraments, and ministry. However, they identified a problematic lack of conversation on certain issues that are fundamental to their ecclesial self-understanding, namely, the relationship between apostolic succession and the Eucharist.[55] Orthodox respondents also identified the need for further dialogue on the relationship between apostolicity and the nature and mission of the church.[56]

One can frame the debates provoked by BEM around the question of "How much can the churches say in common?" Some churches suggested that BEM was too general, arguing that more explicit language should be used. The Lutheran Church–Missouri Synod criticized the document for lacking an explicit hermeneutic. It can be read in too many ways, leaving the churches confused about what they really can say in common.[57] On the other hand, some respondents stressed the danger of attempting to claim too much doctrinal consensus prematurely. For example, the Reformed Church of Hungary made the distinction between a consensus statement and a convergence statement, describing BEM as the latter.[58]

---

[52] The Salvation Army, in Thurian, ed., *Churches Respond to BEM*, vol. 4, 230–35.

[53] Church of Scotland (Reformed), in Thurian, ed., *Churches Respond to BEM*, vol. 1, 96.

[54] Ecumenical Patriarchate of Constantinople, in Thurian, ed., *Churches Respond to BEM*, vol. 4, 4.

[55] Roman Catholic Church, in Thurian, ed., *Churches Respond to BEM*, vol. 6, 7–8.

[56] Inter-Orthodox Symposium, in Thurian, ed., *Churches Respond to BEM*, vol. 1, 126.

[57] Lutheran Church–Missouri Synod, in Thurian, ed., *Churches Respond to BEM*, vol. 3, 132.

[58] Reformed Church of Hungary, in Thurian, ed., *Churches Respond to BEM*, vol. 5, 161.

Regardless of whether or not BEM contains an implicit ecumenical ecclesiology, the unresolved ecclesiological questions in the text (i.e., limits of confessional diversity, as well as structures of ministry that would facilitate shared decision making) beg for further study on the nature and mission of the church. One of the questions that remains significant for ecumenism today is how to relate diversity and unity. This pertains directly to the task of defining the goal of visible unity. The responses to BEM reveal a range of perspectives on the limits of diversity in the unity we seek. The American Baptist Church, among others, stresses that unity does not mean uniformity. They suggest that there needs to be a conversation on how to negotiate diversity in unity.[59] Important questions remain about how to negotiate unity and diversity within the ecumenical movement. These questions are revisited in subsequent conversations about ecclesiology. What are the limits of diversity? How do models of unity in diversity relate to the vision of organic union? Faith and Order took up these questions in a study on the nature of the church as *koinonia* in the years following BEM. *Koinonia* proved to be an important theological principle in envisioning ecumenical ecclesiology.[60] However, it does not resolve all the debates surrounding the nature of the church, nor does it provide a blueprint for how unity in diversity should be articulated and expressed in the ecumenical vision of the WCC.

The understanding of the church as *koinonia* did not begin at BEM. This biblical and theological image of the church as a communion surfaced in ecumenical conversations predating BEM. However, Faith and Order's focus on the church as *koinonia* became sharper in the 1980s. Responding to the invitation to develop ecumenical ecclesiology, Faith and Order focused on *koinonia* to express the reality of the unity we seek. This became a central theme at the WCC's Seventh General Assembly in Canberra (1991). In the Canberra report on the nature of unity, the assembly states:

[59] American Baptist Churches in the USA, in Thurian, ed., *Churches Repond to BEM*, vol. 3, 258.

[60] Following John Zizioulas's understanding of *koinonia*, I am using it to refer to a dynamic ecclesial communion that reflects the inner life of the Trinity. *Koinonia*, from this perspective, frames diversity in unity as it understands communion to emerge out of a shared life together rather than out of uniformity. See John Zizioulas's response to Günther Gassmann in "The Nature and Mission of the Church: Ecumenical Perspectives on Ecclesiology; Background Paper," in Thomas Best, ed., *Faith and Order 1985–1989: The Commission Meeting at Budapest, 1989* (Geneva: WCC, 1989), 209.

> The unity of the church to which we are called is a koinonia given and expressed in the common confession of the apostolic faith; a common sacramental life entered by the one baptism and celebrated together in one eucharistic fellowship; a common life in which members and ministries are mutually recognized and reconciled; and a common mission witnessing to the gospel of God's grace to all people and serving the whole of creation.[61]

This statement on unity became somewhat of a foundation for subsequent conversations on ecclesiology. Faith and Order continued its focus on ecclesiology in preparation for the Fifth World Conference of Faith and Order held in Santiago de Compostela, Spain (1993). Following its theme, "Koinonia in Faith, Life and Witness," the commission studied the nature of *koinonia* and discussed how the concept challenged the churches to fuller unity. In the final report, *On the Way to Fuller Koinonia*, they noted some of the remaining hindrances to full, visible unity among the churches. These include divisions around expressing a common faith and engaging in common witness. These challenges invite the churches to do all that they can to share life and take risks toward recognition of each other's sacraments and ministry. It also invites them to consider how they can promote justice within the church and the world and be a credible sign of unity and peace to a broken world.[62]

The connection between the nature of unity and the promotion of peace and justice was taken up explicitly in the post-Canberra Faith and Order studies related to ecclesiology and ethics. These studies include "Costly Unity" (1993), which stressed the need for the church to always strive to form a moral community, manifesting just relationships within the *koinonia*. "Costly Unity" addressed the concern that the churches were fostering "cheap unity" by forsaking important discussions on ethical issues for the sake of avoiding conflict on controversial issues. "Costly Commitment" (1994) discussed how the church could build unity by fostering cooperative responses to social issues. Finally, "Costly Obedience" (1996) took up more explicitly the nature of the council in relation to the church as an ecclesio-moral communion. These studies invited the council to create space for the development of a moral communion

---

[61] "Canberra 1991: The Unity of the Church as Koinonia: Gift and Calling," in Gassmann, ed., *A Documentary History of Faith and Order*, 4.

[62] Thomas Best and Günther Gassmann, eds., *On the Way to Fuller Koinonia: Official Report of the Fifth World Conference on Faith and Order, Santiago de Compostela, 1993* (Geneva: WCC, 1994), 264–95.

that is not just programmatic but expresses the ecclesial requirements of ethical commitments and action.[63]

The *Ecclesiology and Ethics* studies are important in the discussion on unity because they address the longstanding debate on the orientation of the ecumenical movement. Following the *Unity and Renewal* study, this work brings together the agendas of Faith and Order and Life and Work, highlighting the connection between theological reflection and Christian praxis. The church's ethical action should not be discussed within supplementary programs of the WCC. The church is, by its nature, called to be a moral communion. Therefore, the promotion of unity must be connected to the promotion of peace and justice within the churches and in the world.

The *Ecclesiology and Ethics* studies drew upon *koinonia* as a way to understand the church as a prophetic sign to the world. The idea of *koinonia* provides theological support for the earlier Faith and Order work on the church as a sacrament, an effective sign of God's grace in the world. *Koinonia* speaks of the church's participation in the life of the Trinity. Just as the Trinity is the dynamic reality of divine relationship, the church is a communion of persons who participate in divine life through Christ and his Spirit. While there exists significant disagreement among the churches on how to speak of the holiness of the church,[64] the emphasis on participation in divine life provides a framework for the church as sacrament.

Koinonia also provides a helpful way of talking about the relationship between diversity and unity, which is another key area of discord in ecumenical perspectives on ecclesiology. Orthodox scholar John Zizioulas notes that the Trinity provides the perfect model for unity in diversity. Since it is a dynamic communion of divine persons, it offers a model for relationality.[65] In their responses to BEM, many churches invited a more explicit framework for understanding unity in diversity. It has

---

[63] Thomas Best and Martin Robra, eds., *Ecclesiology and Ethics: Ecumenical Ethical Engagement, Moral Formation and the Nature of the Church* (Geneva: WCC, 1997).

[64] As noted in the *Nature and Mission of the Church* text, some churches refrain from speaking about the church as sinful, while they acknowledge the sinfulness of individual members. For example, the Orthodox emphasizes the holiness of the church and find it unacceptable to talk about the church itself as sinful. On the other hand, there are churches that find it important to name the sinfulness of the church itself, while not denying that God is present within it and continues to sanctify it. See WCC Commission on Faith and Order, *Nature and Mission of the Church*, 33–34.

[65] John of Pergamon, "The Church as Communion: A Presentation on the World Conference Theme," in Best and Gassmann, eds., *On the Way to Fuller Koinonia*, 103–11.

become generally accepted that the unity we seek in the ecumenical movement must be a unity that embraces contextual and, to some extent, confessional diversity. However, the level of acceptable diversity is still a question to which churches offer different responses based on their own ecclesiologies. This conversation reveals continuity with the earlier debates between proponents of organic unity and those who critiqued that model.

This debate on the limits of acceptable diversity was taken up by the Faith and Order Commission in drafting the *Nature and Mission of the Church* text (2005). The text acknowledges that there are divergent perspectives on this issue and urges churches to avoid two extremes. On the one hand, churches should not become so complacent with confessional diversity that they do not take risks to manifest fuller visible unity. On the other hand, churches should not expect a unity that demands stifling uniformity. Such a goal is both unattainable and undesirable. The text identifies this as a significant area of ecclesiological division, stating,

> One of the pressing ecumenical questions is whether and how churches, at this stage of the ecumenical movement, can live in mutual accountability so that they can sustain one another in unity and legitimate diversity, and can prevent new issues from becoming causes of division within and between churches.[66]

This quote identifies two questions that remain challenging in the ecumenical movement. First is the question of how much diversity is acceptable, or, in other words, how much uniformity is desirable. The second and related question is how churches can experience and develop mutual accountability in this stage of the ecumenical movement. The issue of mutual accountability raises questions about the nature of the WCC and other ecumenical organizations, which will be addressed in the next chapter. This issue also begs the question of whether churches can speak with each other and have expectations of each other when they do not have full, visible unity. In other words, what level of recognition and support do we owe to each other as Christians despite the current reality of our divisions?

The Ninth General Assembly in Porto Alegre, Brazil (2006), addressed two of the remaining challenges voiced in *The Nature and Mission of the Church*, namely, how to imagine diversity in unity and how to foster

---

[66] Faith and Order, *Nature and Mission of the Church*, 39.

mutual accountability. In the ecclesiology text, "Called to Be the One Church," they identified the need for churches to continually challenge themselves to deeper relationships of mutual recognition and accountability. This involves each church to acknowledge "all that is provisional in its life and have the courage to acknowledge this to other churches."[67] From this statement, one can see more clearly how the question of mutual accountability relates to the ongoing debate on legitimate diversity. This goes back to the question of the provisional quality of confessional differences and invites the churches to continue dialogues on how much diversity is desirable in the unity that we seek.

The Porto Alegre ecclesiology text makes reference to the church as *koinonia* and connects the image of the triune God with the kind of community that we are called to be. It states that "the church is called to manifest its oneness in rich diversity."[68] Remaining debates about what unity in diversity looks like points to the fact that *koinonia*, while helpful, does not provide a blueprint for the unity we seek. It is important to note that the use of *koinonia* in ecumenical conversations did not resolve all challenges in the area of ecclesiology. While *koinonia* proved to be a rich concept for ecumenical ecclesiology, some flagged the danger of overemphasizing one understanding of the church over all others.[69] The fact of ecclesiological plurality is one that we cannot ignore in the ecumenical movement. This invites us to consider the principles of the Toronto statement as we continue conversations on the nature of visible unity.

OPENNESS TO THE ESCHATOLOGICAL REALITY OF UNITY

The focus on ecclesiology in the past twenty-five years has revealed an incredible diversity of the self-understandings among member and/or participant churches in the World Council of Churches. From Orthodox and Roman Catholic churches that emphasize church unity in visible structures to the Quakers and Baptist churches that emphasize church unity in an invisible communion, the range of ecclesiological diversity is vast. When we think of the church as *koinonia*, this diversity can be regarded as an integral part of the dynamic reality of relationality. At the

---

[67] General Assembly at Porto Alegre, "Called to Be the One Church," *The Ecumenical Review* 58, nos. 1–2 (January–April 2006): 114.

[68] General Assembly at Porto Alegre, "Called to Be the One Church," 113.

[69] Mary O'Driscoll, "Thoughts on the Ecclesiology Text," in Alan Falconer, ed., *Faith and Order in Moshi: The 1996 Commission Meeting* (Geneva: WCC, 1998), 109–14.

same time, ecclesiological differences complicate the task of articulating a common vision of the unity we seek as Christian churches. We still experience questions around the limits of diversity and appropriateness of uniformity. We also face the question of how to foster mutual account-ability within the divisions that still remain.

In many ways, the inclusivity of the WCC testifies to the success of the Toronto statement. We recall the attentiveness to diversity that charac-terized the early leaders in the WCC such as Visser 't Hooft. His vision of the WCC as a space that could foster ecumenical dialogue and activity among diverse Christian churches gave life to the Toronto statement. Sixty years later, we are even more aware of the diverse ecclesiologies present in the ecumenical movement. The Toronto statement's open-ness to ecclesiological diversity strikes us as even more relevant today as we face the challenge of pursuing Christian unity within the reality of ambiguity on the nature of that unity.

The contemporary significance of the Toronto statement has been challenged in recent years. During the preparatory studies on the nature and mission of the church, the Toronto statement emerged as a point of contention. Some argued that the Toronto statement was outdated and that it actually hindered dialogue on ecclesiology. For example, John Zizioulas claimed that the Toronto statement has been used as an excuse to avoid the topic of ecclesiology.[70] From this perspective, upholding neutrality as a positive value rather than a provisional stance is a mistake because it allows churches to be complacent in the face of divisions in the area of ecclesiology. Responding to concerns that the Toronto statement is outdated, Vitaly Borovoy argues that the Toronto statement should be credited with opening the space for ecclesiological diversity. With its commitment to openness, the Toronto statement has prevented the WCC from becoming overly institutionalized, a process that would have alienated Roman Catholic, Orthodox, and Free Churches.[71]

---

[70] John Zizioulas's response to Günther Gassmann, "The Nature and Mission of the Church: Ecumenical Perspectives on Ecclesiology; Background Paper," in Tomas Best, ed., *Faith and Order 1985–1989*, 209.

[71] Vitaly Borovoy, "The Ecclesiological Significance of the WCC: The Legacy and Promise of Toronto," in *The Ecumenical Review* 40, nos. 3–4 (July–Oct 1988): 504–18. I will discuss these debates around the Toronto statement in the next chapter, as the statement relates more directly to the questions around the ecclesiological status of the WCC and its role within the ecumenical movement. The Toronto statement also pertains to the question of unity and how ecclesiology influences different perspectives, which is relevant to this particular conversation.

Convinced that we must remain open to the nature of Christian unity for the sake of inclusivity, I argue that the Toronto statement is still relevant today. The reality of ecclesiological plurality and ambiguity surrounding the nature of unity makes the principles of the Toronto statement even more appropriate for our contemporary context. In this section, I will address some of the objections to the Toronto statement using Habermas's insights on how to facilitate consensus through honest and dominance-free discourse. Ultimately, I argue that unity should be understood eschatologically, not definitively, serving to regulate our dialogue and action even though it is ultimately a mystery that cannot be fully grasped as yet.

Critics of the Toronto statement have suggested that the WCC should not remain completely neutral with respect to the nature of unity because of the history of conversations on the topic. These conversations, particularly on the topic of ecclesiology, should inform the WCC's conception of unity, thus allowing the council to articulate more explicitly the goal of ecumenism. Stated succinctly, the question at hand here is whether open-endedness on the nature of unity should be regarded as a positive value in itself. Should we consider the Toronto statement to be a time-bound articulation of where the council was in the 1950s, or should it be considered a principle to regulate the self-understanding of the WCC and its approach to the unity question?

Habermas's distinction between strategic and communicative action sheds light on these questions. First, recall that Habermas assumes that the goal of a communicative encounter will shape the way the interlocutors approach the whole conversation. Building on this assumption, he distinguishes between communicative action and strategic action. Communicative action is characterized by the pursuit of mutual understanding, which is built into the rational structure of communicative competence. Strategic action occurs when communicators aim at secondary goals that are either disclosed or undisclosed and that hinder the free pursuit of rational agreement.[72]

Applied specifically to the context of ecumenical dialogue, the theory can help us understand the connection between the way we imagine unity and our approach to ecumenical dialogue. If the World Council of Churches presupposes a model of unity, thus framing the goal of ecu-

---

[72] Jürgen Habermas, "Actions, Speech Acts, Linguistically Mediated Interactions and Lifeworld," in Maeve Cooke, ed., *On the Pragmatics of Communication* (Cambridge, MA: MIT Press, 1998), 220–27.

menical dialogue, it can hinder the freedom of the conversation. Using insights from Habermas's theory of communicative action, I argue that the Toronto statement was insightful in its designation of neutrality on the unity question. Visser 't Hooft's insistence on openness to the question of unity and ecclesiological neutrality within the WCC was correct at the time and is valuable today.

If, for example, the model of organic unity is prioritized by the council, churches that do not find resonance with this model could be either marginalized or manipulated in the pursuit of Christian unity. The history of debates on the nature of unity reveals significant disagreements on the appropriateness of this model for all churches. Furthermore, these disagreements are grounded in the very self-understandings of the churches. Studies in ecclesiology have highlighted some divisive issues that still need to be addressed before common statements on the nature and mission of the church can be made. This fact serves to illustrate that the ecclesiological pluralism to which the Toronto statement spoke is still present and perhaps even more apparent than in 1950.

Some would argue that we have reached significant understanding on the nature of unity so that we are able to frame the goal out of a common agreement. While the progress toward mutual understanding should not be ignored, it is also important to recognize that understandings are always changing. The self-understanding of the Catholic Church, for example, has developed significantly in the past century, particularly in response to the theological developments at the Second Vatican Council. The Catholic Church's approach to ecclesiology and, along with that, to Christian unity has shifted in focus since the formation of the WCC. Even if the goal of a conversation is framed in common language and mutual understanding, it is still valuable to maintain openness to the possibility of development. It is particularly valuable when differences are so deeply grounded in one's ecclesial self-understanding.

Another concern that has been raised with respect to the applicability of the Toronto statement in ecumenical dialogue today pertains to the fear of relativism. Does openness to the nature of unity imply that all understandings of unity are equally true and appropriate? Again, Habermas's theory is helpful here. We recall that he develops his theory of communicative rationality as a way to avoid both positivism and relativism. His critique of postmodern thought includes a rejection of relativism as an epistemological stance. We can observe his distrust of relativism in his theory of communicative action in a couple of ways that are relevant for this conversation as well. First, Habermas argues that the very act of raising a truth claim submits it to a process of validation. Second, he presents a multidimensional understanding of truth that corresponds to different kinds of legitimation. So, a claim to objective truth requires a different level of consensus for validation than a claim to subjective truthfulness.[73]

What does this mean for ecumenical dialogue? For one thing, it provides theoretical support for long-standing ecumenical wisdom that invites churches to recognize that some truths are more necessary to hold in common than others. Different traditions teach this principle in various ways. Illustrating this concept, the Catholic Church invites us to consider that there exists a hierarchy of truths. The Second Vatican Council implores us to remember the hierarchy of truths when engaging in ecumenical dialogue. *Unitatis Redintegratio*, Vatican II's Decree on Ecumenism, states, "When comparing doctrines with one another they [Catholic theologians] should remember that in Catholic doctrine there exists an order or 'hierarchy' of truths, since they vary in their relation to the foundation of the Christian faith" (UR 11). Some truth claims are more integral to the Christian faith than others, and many of these core beliefs are held in common with other Christian communities. This is important to consider as we discern the limits of diversity in unity. Certain truth claims invite a higher level of consensus than others. Habermas suggests that truth claims need to be validated by everyone affected. Using this logic, I argue that those claims that are foundational to the Christian faith should be accepted by all Christians, while those claims that are only integral to a particular church do not need to be recognized by all in order to be considered valid.

How do Christians discern a hierarchy of truths together? This is an important question because the significance of a particular faith claim is shaped by the tradition out of which it emerges. Going back to the nature of religious validity claims that I developed in chapter 1, I argue that the process of reaching mutual understanding must be ongoing. Religious validity claims are narrative expressions of a particular community and can only be understood through a process of coming to know that community. A common language may emerge through the exchange of particular narratives, but it should not be assumed prior to the dialogue.

A related concern that influenced the Toronto statement and has surfaced in different ways throughout the history of the council is that

---

[73] Jürgen Habermas, *Truth and Justification*, edited and translated by Barbara Fultner (Cambridge, MA: MIT Press, 2003), 256–61.

churches will sacrifice their particular truth claims for the sake of unity. The Orthodox and Roman Catholic churches, in particular, have voiced the concern that visible unity will be promoted at the expense of the doctrinal purity that they believe to have been upheld in their respective traditions. Similarly, we see the concern that churches will sacrifice commitments to social justice for the sake of "cheap unity." Both of these concerns point to the fear that unity will result in a loss of one's commitment to a particular truth. Recall that the Toronto statement's commitment to neutrality is actually for the sake of particular truth claims. The WCC remains neutral on the nature of unity so that the topic can be discussed from diverse ecclesiological perspectives. Churches are not asked to give up their ecclesial self-understandings in order to be members in the council. This goes so far as to include churches that cannot fully acknowledge the ecclesial status of other churches.

Habermas's theory supports and challenges this position in a couple of ways. Habermas acknowledges the embeddedness of knowledge through his understanding of the lifeworld. Furthermore, he argues that the immediacy of social integration within the lifeworld should be protected against the infringement of systemic steering media. From this perspective, the particularity of truth claims coming out of the taken-for-granted knowledge of a lifeworld or, analogously, the lived tradition of a particular church should be protected against the influence of an institution. At the same time, Habermas argues that when people realize that their lifeworld knowledge is relative to their location and have to address the reality of pluralism, explicit discourse is required.[74] Ecumenical encounters similarly invite churches to acknowledge the contextual (not neutral) nature of their truth claims in the face of confessional diversity. Using Habermas's insights, I argue that dialogue does not require the abandonment of one's truth claims. Rather, it invites an exchange of truth claims through the process of discourse.

Habermas articulates rules of discourse to ensure that rationality is the binding force of an agreement. This disallows coercive and exclusionary means of creating consensus. Recall that Habermas's discourse theory articulates that everyone affected by the outcome of a discourse must be able to freely agree on the rationality of that discourse.[75] In other words,

[74] Habermas, "Actions, Speech Acts, Linguistically Mediated Interactions, and Lifeworld," in Cooke, ed., *On the Pragmatics of Communication*, 233–55.

[75] Habermas, "The Architectonics of Discursive Differentiation," in *Between Naturalism and Religion*, trans. Ciaran Cronin (Malden, MA: Polity Press, 2008), 82.

they must be able to say yes or no to the validity of the truth claims raised in the discourse. The process of reaching consensus is always ongoing. Habermas suggests that consensus serves more as a regulative principle for the process of discourse than as an achievable outcome of real-life communication. Recall Seyla Benhabib's critical reading of Habermas, which invites more attention to the real-life implications of his theory. She argues that an abstract ideal of consensus is not necessary for Habermas's principles of discourse to effectively regulate a communicative encounter.[76] The abstract quality of Habermas's discourse theory invites a concrete application of it.

Applied to ecumenical dialogue, Habermas's theory of discourse offers several insights. As I have already stated, freedom and inclusivity are ensured by openness to ecclesiological pluralism. Churches must be able to raise truth claims about the nature of unity out of the particularity of their own tradition. Furthermore, it is necessary to consider a hierarchy of truths when determining the level of consensus required for a truth claim to be acceptable within the limits of diversity in unity. Finally, consensus serves as a regulative principle for the process of dialogue itself. Therefore, the success of the ecumenical encounter cannot be measured solely by the goal of visible unity, but it must take into consideration the unifying effects of the communicative process itself.

The final point is perhaps the most significant for the ecumenical context today. Many ecumenists have noted a lack of ecumenical enthusiasm or an indifference to the promotion of visible unity. Some have attributed this ecumenical climate to the ambiguity surrounding the goal. In other words, they argue that a clearer understanding of the nature of visible unity might promote more active and inclusive participation in the ecumenical movement. However, the reality of plurality and ambiguity will not go away in a postmodern context. This reality compels us to promote ecumenical participation and enthusiasm without a clearly defined goal. Theoretically, one can argue that it is due to the always open-ended reality of consensus. Theologically, one can argue that it is due to the eschatological nature of the Christian church.

Stated in a variety of ways throughout the history of the ecumenical movement, the eschatological reality of the church necessitates the acceptance that the ultimate unity that we seek will come as a gift from

---

[76] Benhabib, *Situating the Self: Gender, Community and Postmodernism in Contemporary Ethics* (New York: Routledge, 1992), 26–38.

God and not as a result of human efforts. From a Christian theological perspective, history is always understood within an eschatological frame-work, with a view toward the final consummation of all things in God. This perspective invites us to labor for unity with the knowledge that our efforts are never enough. Even if we do not reach full, visible unity in history, Christ's prayer that we may all be one compels us to continue working for that reality. The ideal of full, visible unity, like the ideal of consensus, can inform and motivate the process of ecumenical dialogue, but it remains, to some extent, an ideal that we cannot fully achieve in history.

Letty Russell highlights the eschatological nature of the church in her work on ecclesiology entitled *Church in the Round*. Russell presents an ideal image of the church as a roundtable, emphasizing the qualities of inclusivity and egalitarianism. She contrasts this with the church that we experience, noting our failures in history to be one, holy, catholic, and apostolic. Using the framework of the church as a sign of the reign of God, she articulates an eschatological ecclesiology. She states, "*Church in the Round* describes a community of faith and struggle working to an-ticipate God's New Creation by becoming partners with those who are at the margins of church and society."[77] The church is a real but imperfect sign of the fullness of God's presence. Specifically referring to the unity of the church, oneness is a mark that we must live into now but with the knowledge that it will come in its fullness at the end of history.

The eschatological reality of the church is emphasized in different ways from different ecclesial self-understandings. In a Roman Catholic context, the eschatological reality of the church is highlighted in the image of the church as a pilgrim community. Lifted up in a particular way at the Second Vatican Council, the image of the church as a pil-grim community stresses the constant invitation for all members of the church to grow in holiness through ongoing conversion to Christ. This understanding of the church shapes Catholic approaches to ecumenism. John Paul II emphasized the need for all participants in the ecumenical movement to place their focus on growing toward Christ. Growing closer to Christ will allow the churches to grow in visible unity since Christ is the one source of unity in the Church. Echoing John Paul II, Walter Kasper suggests that spiritual ecumenism should be the foundation of all

---

[77] See Letty Russell, *Church in the Round: Feminist Interpretation of the Church* (Louisville: Westminster John Knox Press, 1993), 12.

efforts to promote Christian unity. Spiritual ecumenism involves personal and ecclesial growth in holiness through deepening one's relationship to Christ. It requires a "conversion of heart," which can only be achieved through prayer and acceptance of God's promise of grace.[78]

The theological understanding of the church as an eschatological reality invites us to ecumenical hope and commitment. From a Habermasian perspective, it serves as a regulative principle for ecumenical dialogue, just as the ideal of consensus provides a framework for discourse. Within this approach, ecumenical enthusiasm comes not from clarity about the nature of the goal but from a sure hope that the goal of Christian unity is as certain as its source. Visser 't Hooft expressed confidence in the unity of the church as an eschatological reality during the formative period of the World Council of Churches. This hope is the foundation of the Toronto statement, which insists that the WCC remain open with respect to the nature of unity.

Reading the Toronto statement through the lens of Habermas's theory of communicative action allows us to appreciate the statement's contemporary relevance in addressing the question of the unity we seek. The question needs to be an open-ended one, allowing the churches to freely and honestly articulate responses from within their own ecclesial self-understandings. This position of neutrality informs how the World Council of Churches understands itself and its own role in the ecumenical movement. The next chapter will take up debates on the nature of the World Council of Churches. Again drawing upon the principles of the Toronto statement and using a critical appropriation of Habermas's theory to identify its contemporary relevance, I will address the major areas of disagreement surrounding the nature of the WCC and its role in the ecumenical movement. These debates are particularly relevant today within discussions of how the WCC can create space for wider participation in its ecumenical work and how the shift to the consensus model of deliberation in the WCC has necessitated a reflection on the ethos of the WCC.

---

[78] For example, see John Paul II, *Ut Unam Sint*, and Walter Kasper's recent statement, "The Ecumenical Movement in the 21st Century," a presentation at the event marking the fortieth anniversary of the Joint Working Group between the Roman Catholic Church and the WCC (2005).

4

The Future of Ecumenism
and the World Council of Churches

The Toronto statement provoked conversations on two key topics pertaining to the nature of membership in the World Council of Churches. The previous chapter explored debates around the nature of unity and the ecclesiological stance of the WCC. This chapter will take up the second conversation surrounding the Toronto statement, namely, the nature of the World Council of Churches and its role in the ecumenical movement. The WCC has located itself within the larger ecumenical movement by acknowledging that it is one instrument among others dedicated to the promotion of Christian unity. At the same time, given its inclusivity and historical prominence, the World Council of Churches is in a unique position within the ecumenical movement, which should be considered in determining its nature and mission. This observation is made in the 1997 Faith and Order text entitled "Toward a Common Understanding and Vision of the World Council of Churches" (CUV). The Faith and Order Commission states:

> While the ecumenical movement is wider than its organizational expressions, and while the WCC is essentially the fellowship of its member churches, it serves at the same time as a prominent instrument and expression of the ecumenical movement. As such it is an advocate of the impulse for renewal which has characterized the movement from its beginnings.[1]

Considering the historical prominence of the WCC within the movement toward Christian unity, the significance of the nature and mission

---

[1] WCC Commission on Faith and Order, "Toward a Common Understanding and Vision of the World Council of Churches," in *Assembly Workbook for Harare 1998* (Geneva: WCC, 1998), 103.

of the WCC extends beyond its member churches. With that in mind, this chapter will highlight debates on the nature and mission of the WCC and explore their contemporary relevance for the larger ecumenical movement.

During the 1990s, the Toronto statement was revisited and its relevance was debated in preparation for the Faith and Order study "Toward a Common Understanding and Vision of the World Council of Churches." The Faith and Order Commission raised questions about the nature of the council and its relationship to the one church of Christ, the ability of the WCC to speak on behalf of its member churches, decision-making procedures within the council, and the possibility of creating space within the council for broader participation with others in the larger ecumenical movement. These questions, which pertain to the nature and mission of the WCC, have implications on recent conversations around the decision-making processes of the council and the shift toward a consensus model of deliberation, as well as conversations about creating a space for broader participation within the council and greater collaboration with other ecumenical visions.

Exploring these conversations through the lens of contemporary critical theory offers a theoretical support for the Toronto statement and a rationale behind the WCC's movement toward a consensus model of deliberation and a broadened space for inclusive ecumenical participation beyond member churches. Specifically, I argue that the insights of Jürgen Habermas on facilitating discourse in modern pluralistic societies can inform the self-understanding of the World Council of Churches as it endeavors to locate itself as a forum for dominance-free, inclusive dialogue among diverse Christian communities. This chapter will take up the Toronto statement again with the intention of highlighting the issues around the nature of membership in the council and the role of the WCC in the larger ecumenical movement. This exploration will highlight several questions that have contemporary relevance. What is the relationship between the WCC and the ecumenical councils of the early church? How can the WCC promote dominance-free dialogue with minority churches in the council? How can the WCC collaborate with nonmember churches in promoting Christian unity?

THE TORONTO STATEMENT
AND THE FORMATIVE YEARS OF THE WCC

The existence of the World Council of Churches expresses a contradiction, or at least a tension, that defines the ecumenical movement. On the one hand, the council exists because of the unity of Christians. As stated in the WCC's basis, "The World Council of Churches is a fellowship of churches which confess the Lord Jesus Christ as God and Savior."[2] This common profession of faith as well as a shared baptism provides a foundation for Christians to recognize the real unity that exists among them. In other words, the ecumenical movement rests on the realization that there is a common foundation and calling that all Christians share. On the other hand, the ecumenical movement exists because there is disunity among Christians. If we had full Christian unity, we would not need a movement to promote it. The World Council of Churches serves the cause of Christian unity, which is not yet fully manifested.

This tension has framed discussions around the nature of the WCC. During the formative years of the WCC, debates ensued around how to talk about the relationship between the World Council of Churches and the church of Christ, the *Una Sancta*, the "one, holy, catholic, and apostolic church" of which the Nicene-Constantinopolitan Creed speaks. The *Una Sancta* is the church that Christians believe in and strive to manifest. The Creed lists "oneness" or Christian unity as a feature of the *Una Sancta*. Considering the incompleteness of unity, which the ecumenical movement addresses, one cannot identify the WCC with the *Una Sancta* itself.

Although the WCC is not the "one, holy, catholic and apostolic church" of the Christian faith, the WCC is a real, inclusive fellowship of Christians and thus, provides a space for shared life and common witness. The unity manifested in the shared life and common witness of the WCC should not be dismissed as insignificant. At the same time, the World Council of Churches is not a full expression of unity and does not manifest conciliarity to the same degree as the early councils of the Church.[3] In other words, since the WCC is not an expression of full, visible unity but an expression of incomplete unity that acknowledges that greater unity can be manifested, it cannot speak with the same level

---

[2] Willem A. Visser 't Hooft, ed., *The First Assembly of the World Council of Churches* (New York: Harper and Brothers, 1949), 197.

[3] In this context, I understand conciliarity to refer to the expression of ecclesial unity through assemblies that have the authority to speak on behalf of the local churches represented. For a discussion of conciliarity, see "The Unity of the Church—the Next Steps: Report of the Salamanca Consultation Convened by the Faith and Order Commission, WCC on 'Concepts of Unity and Models of Union' Sept. 1973," in WCC Commission on Faith and Order, *What Kind of Unity?* (Geneva: WCC, 1974).

of ecclesial authority as the early ecumenical councils. So, how should the World Council of Churches speak and with what level of authority?

The Toronto statement addressed this question by explicitly stating that the WCC should not be regarded in any way as a superchurch. By declaring the WCC's nonecclesial status, the Central Committee at Toronto stressed that the World Council of Churches is not the one church of Christ that they seek in the ecumenical movement. Rather, it is an instrument to foster unity among the churches themselves, and it is only authoritative in so much as it serves this function for the churches. The text states this succinctly:

> It is not a Super-Church. It is not the World Church. It is not the *Una Sancta* of which the Creeds speak. This misunderstanding arises again and again although it has been denied as clearly as possible in official pronouncements of the Council. It is based on complete ignorance of the real situation within the Council. For if the Council should in any way violate its own constitutional principle, that it cannot legislate or act for its member Churches, it would cease to maintain the support of its membership.[4]

If the WCC is not the *Una Sancta*, to what degree does it manifest an ecclesial reality? This question was raised and debated in response to the Toronto statement. The debate did not center so much on the appropriateness of the Toronto statement in delineating what the council *is not*. Disagreements ensued around the question of whether a more positive statement could be drafted to declare what the council actually *is*. This emerged again in the 1990s when the WCC drafted "Toward a Common Understanding and Vision of the World Council of Churches." The foundation for subsequent conversations is found within the formative years of the WCC and responses to the Toronto statement. It is worth examining these conversations, therefore, as they provide a foundation for analyzing the contemporary debate.

Once again, Visser 't Hooft was a prominent voice in the conversations surrounding the ecclesiological significance of the WCC during the formative years of the council. He argued that the World Council of Churches was a unique reality in Christian history and merited care-

---

[4] WCC Central Committee at Toronto 1950, "The Church, the Churches and the World Council of Churches: The Ecclesiological Significance of the World Council of Churches," in Lukas Vischer, ed., *A Documentary History of the Faith and Order Movement 1927–1963* (St. Louis, MO: Bethany Press, 1963), 169.

ful explanation of its nature and purpose. From the beginning, Visser 't Hooft maintained that the council should not be conceived as a purely administrative organization because of the way in which it provided the opportunity for common witness among the churches.[5] Specifically, the WCC allows the churches to manifest their unity in a very real and visible way through shared prayer, worship, and service. In this respect, it does not just facilitate Christian unity but also reveals a significant level of Christian unity that already exists in shared faith and baptism.

Following the ecclesiology of Karl Barth, which separates the institutional manifestation of the church from events of the church manifested in history,[6] Visser 't Hooft argued that the WCC could not be identified with the *Una Sancta*, and yet it should not be denied that the WCC can manifest the *Una Sancta* within history when it manifests the Body of Christ in the world. Visser 't Hooft stated that "The World Council of Churches must, therefore, not pretend that it represents the *Una Sancta* but it may and it must claim that it is a body in which and through which, when it pleases God, the *Una Sancta* becomes manifest."[7]

The implicit ecclesiology behind Visser 't Hooft's perspective is evident in discussions surrounding the Toronto statement. Visser 't Hooft argued that since the WCC was not the *Una Sancta*, it must be regarded as a provisional entity. He explicitly stated that the WCC must be willing to die away in order to allow the true *Una Sancta* to be manifested in history.[8] The provisional character of the WCC as advocated by Visser 't Hooft and others was a subject of debate in the formative years of the council. Responding to Visser 't Hooft's paper, "The World Council of Churches: Its Nature—Its Limits," US theologian Henry Van Dusen critiqued the assertion that the WCC was necessarily provisional. He

---

[5] Willem A. Visser 't Hooft, *The Genesis and Formation of the World Council of Churches* (Geneva: WCC, 1982), 63–69.

[6] Barth argued that the church was manifested in history when two or three were gathered faithfully to the Gospel. He said that the institutional church could manifest the true church in moments, but the institutional church should not be identified as the true church. In this way, Barth held the church as institution accountable to the *Una Sancta* that we believe in. Visser 't Hooft was influenced by Barthian ecclesiology, and this is reflected in his position on the ecclesial status of the WCC. See Jerome Hamer, "What is the World Council of Churches in Its Own Theological View?" in *Istina* no. 4 (1954).

[7] Willem A. Visser 't Hooft, "The World Council of Churches: Its Nature—Its Limits," (First Draft) Study 47E/102A, March 1947 (Geneva: World Council of Churches Study Dept., 1947), 19–20.

[8] Ibid.

suggested that this understanding was pessimistic in that it limited the real potential of the WCC to manifest the fullness of Christian unity. He noted that "some [churches] think that the World Council of Churches expresses the form which the unity of Christ is ultimately to take."[9] Van Dusen suggested that a pessimistic understanding of the WCC does not sufficiently acknowledge the potential of the council to manifest more fully the unity that we seek in the ecumenical movement. From his perspective, emphasis on the provisional status of the WCC diminished its significance as a manifestation of Christian unity and diminished its authority to speak on behalf of the member churches.[10]

The question of whether the WCC can speak on behalf of its member churches sparked a revealing debate about the nature of the council. Visser 't Hooft argued that the WCC could not speak with the same level of authority as a church since the WCC itself lacked the ecclesial status of an early Christian council. The WCC has authority only in so much as the churches recognize the *Una Sancta* within it. Again, from Visser 't Hooft's perspective, the *Una Sancta* is manifested in moments of authentic witness and not perpetually through the WCC as an institution. Others, such as Van Dusen, argued that the WCC needed to be able to speak on behalf of the member churches in order to manifest a prophetic Christian witness.[11] The question of whether the WCC has the authority to speak on behalf of its member churches would return at different moments in the history of the council. Some argue that with its size and inclusivity, the World Council of Churches is in a unique position to mobilize Christian churches for service and articulate a prophetic Christian vision of social justice. One of the most notable examples of the WCC exercising its influence in the promotion of justice was its denouncement of apartheid in South Africa.[12]

[9] Van Dusen, quoted in *Minutes and Reports of the Third Meeting of the Central Committee of the World Council of Churches Toronto, July 9–15, 1950* (Geneva: WCC), 15.

[10] Willem A. Visser 't Hooft lays out the arguments for and against the provisional status of the WCC in *The Genesis and Formation of the World Council of Churches* (Geneva: WCC, 1982), 72–85.

[11] Commentary on Willem A. Visser 't Hooft, "The World Council of Churches: Its Nature—Its Limits," in the same volume, 34–35.

[12] For a discussion of the WCC's involvement in opposing apartheid in South Africa, which offers an important example of the WCC utilizing its global significance to promote social activism, see Pauline Webb, ed., *A Long Struggle: The Involvement of the World Council of Churches in South Africa* (Geneva: WCC, 1994).

The real issue at hand in the discussion on the WCC's authority to speak for the churches pertains to the disputed level of mutual recognition implied in membership in the council. The concept of mutual recognition, in this context, refers to whether churches acknowledge the ecclesial status of each other. The question of mutual recognition has been raised in multiple contexts throughout the history of the WCC. Put succinctly, should churches have to acknowledge the ecclesial status of other churches in order to participate in the WCC? This question is essentially ecclesiological because a church's ecclesial self-understanding shapes the way that it perceives the ecclesial status of other churches. Therefore, ecclesiological diversity demands a careful consideration of the implications of mutual recognition.

The Toronto statement emphasized the legitimacy of ecclesiological diversity when it did not make mutual recognition a requirement for membership in the WCC. It states:

> The member churches of the World Council consider the relationship of other churches to the Holy Catholic Church which the Creeds profess as a subject for mutual consideration. Nevertheless, membership does not imply that each church must regard the other member churches as churches in the true and full sense of the word. There is a place in the World Council both for those churches which recognize other churches as churches in the full and true sense, and for those which do not. But these divided churches, even if they cannot yet accept each other as true and pure churches, believe that they should not remain in isolation from each other, and consequently they have associated themselves in the World Council of Churches.[13]

I interpret this text as offering flexibility for the sake of including churches that, for ecclesiological reasons, cannot recognize the full ecclesial status of others. Flexibility does not mean complacency, as the text challenges churches to discern what their common profession of faith means.

Again, we hear Visser 't Hooft's influence in the conversation, for he stressed the need for openness on the ecclesiological question of mutual recognition. He argued that membership in the council needed to be open to churches—particularly in consideration of the Orthodox—whose ecclesiologies disallowed them from acknowledging the reality of the church outside of their tradition. He noted that if mutual recognition were a

---

[13] WCC Central Committee at Toronto, "The Church, the Churches and the World Council of Churches," in Vischer, *A Documentary History*, 173.

prerequisite for membership in the council, the Orthodox and Roman Catholic churches, in particular, could be marginalized from the WCC. Visser 't Hooft did not purport this to be the ideal of Christian unity; rather, he saw it as a reality of the disunity that necessitates an ecumenical movement in the first place.[14] In the drafting of the Toronto statement, it was noted that "the WCC as a matter of fact has only been possible at all just because it has included those who "unchurch" each other."[15]

At the same time, concerns were raised that this position would allow the churches to become complacent in their disunity. The discussions surrounding the drafting of the Toronto statement reveal the fear that accepting the absence of mutual recognition from its member churches would perpetuate divisions within the church of Christ. One of the most vocal opponents to confusing ecclesiological openness with complacency of division was Bishop Newbigin. He continually pushed the Central Committee to consider the Toronto statement as a starting point to articulate what the WCC *is not*, but not as a positive statement on what the WCC actually *is*. He argued against Visser 't Hooft that ecclesiological neutrality should not be considered a positive value in itself and that the council needs to continually move toward articulating a positive statement on ecclesiology, which would necessitate mutual recognition among member churches.[16]

The Toronto statement reflects these concerns to some degree in articulating the expectation of some level of mutual recognition. Again, the Toronto statement is careful to invite the churches to a greater level of unity without making demands that might detour certain churches from joining the WCC. Listing the assumptions held by the WCC with regard to membership in the council, the text states that

> the member churches of the World Council recognize in other churches elements of the true Church. They consider that this mutual recognition obliges them to enter into a serious conversation with each other in the hope that these elements of truth will lead to the recognition of the full truth and to unity based on the full truth. . . . Questions may and must be raised about the validity and purity of teaching and sacramental life, but there can be no question that such dynamic elements of church life justify the hope that the churches which maintain them

---

[14] Visser 't Hooft, "The World Council of Churches: Its Nature—Its Limits," 21.

[15] Dr. Baille, in the *Minutes and Reports of the Third Meeting of the Central Committee of the World Council of Churches Toronto, July 9–15, 1950* (Geneva: WCC, 1950), 17.

[16] Visser 't Hooft, *The Genesis and Formation of the WCC*, 80.

will be led into fuller truth. It is through the ecumenical conversation that this recognition of truth is facilitated.[17]

The Toronto statement invites churches to recognize elements of the true church outside of their own church as a given in their ecumenical commitment. At the same time, commentators would note that the Toronto statement remains open on ecclesiological questions. As we shall see in the next section, some respondents critique the Toronto statement for failing to articulate a positive statement on the ecclesiological significance of the WCC. Proponents of this position suggest that the Toronto statement responded to a historical need that no longer defines the ecumenical situation. In the years surrounding the development of the CUV text, the Toronto statement was lifted up and debated again. Many of the conversations reflected the issues that were raised in the formative years of the WCC.

RECENT DEBATES ON THE TORONTO STATEMENT

When the Faith and Order Commission made ecclesiology a primary focus of their work after *Baptism, Eucharist and Ministry* (1982), the Toronto statement resurfaced as a topic of conversation. The debates on the Toronto statement were particularly significant within two studies that occurred in the post-BEM era of the WCC, namely, *The Nature and Mission of the Church: On the Way to a Common Statement* and "Toward a Common Understanding and Vision of the World Council of Churches" (CUV). Drawing upon recent studies on the ecclesiological significance of *koinonia*, the *Nature and Mission of the Church* text sought to articulate an ecumenical ecclesiology more explicitly. As one can imagine, the Toronto statement was revisited because of its admonitions to refrain from defining a guiding ecclesiology for the work of the WCC. In the CUV text, the Faith and Order Commission sought to articulate the nature and mission of the WCC within the contemporary ecumenical era. Once again, the Toronto statement proved to be significant because of the way in which it laid out the assumptions about the council in the formative years, particularly as it described what the WCC is not. During the drafting of the CUV text, it was argued that the council needed to go beyond

---

[17] WCC Central Committee at Toronto, "The Church, the Churches and the World Council of Churches," in Vischer, *A Documentary History*, 174.

Toronto in asserting a more positive declaration about what exactly the WCC is within the broader context of the one ecumenical movement.

In the preparation for the background paper for the *Nature and Mission of the Church* text, the question was raised as to whether the Toronto statement was outdated for the conversation. Jose Bonino argued this position, stating that the Toronto statement provided a good foundation for the WCC as it emphasized openness and inclusivity. However, he also advocated for a deeper exploration of the ecclesial significance of the WCC, suggesting that the Toronto statement does not say enough about what the WCC is, only what it is not.[18] Others, such as Thomas Stransky, echoed Bonino's suggestion that the Toronto statement fails to make a positive statement on the nature and mission of the WCC, that it simply delineates what the WCC is not.[19]

For those who advocated for the WCC to go beyond the Toronto statement in its articulation of a common self-understanding and vision, there was a perceived awareness of the need for greater clarity on the vision of the council. They argued that the council had reached a greater level of consensus on the common ecclesiological assumptions among its member churches through the ecclesiology studies since *Baptism, Eucharist and Ministry*. This was made explicit by Vitaly Borovoy, who argued that the studies on the church as *koinonia* provided a solid foundation for articulating the ecclesial significance of the WCC. He argued that churches were ready to move beyond Toronto in developing an ecumenical ecclesiology.[20]

Although the Toronto statement was initially drafted out of concern for including churches other than mainstream Protestants in the WCC, these churches were among those that declared the statement to be outdated. From an Orthodox perspective, John Zizioulas suggested that "ecclesiology is both omnipresent and absent in ecumenical dialogues"[21] and that the Toronto statement was used as an excuse for churches to avoid difficult conversations about ecclesiological differences. In preparation for the *Nature and Mission of the Church* study, Zizioulas suggested that the

---

[18] Vitaly Borovoy, "The Ecclesiological Significance of the WCC: The Legacy and Promise of Toronto," *The Ecumenical Review* 40, nos. 3–4 (July–Oct 1988): 513.

[19] Ibid.

[20] Ibid., 512.

[21] Günther Gassmann, "The Nature and Mission of the Church: Ecumenical Perspectives on Ecclesiology; Background Paper," in Thomas Best, ed., *Faith and Order 1985–1989: The Commission Meeting at Budapest, 1989* (Geneva: WCC, 1989), 209.

churches needed to move beyond the Toronto statement's neutrality on ecclesiological questions.[22] Furthermore, Borovoy suggests that some Evangelicals have found the Toronto statement to be a hindrance from moving forward toward greater collaboration with the WCC in the ecumenical movement.[23] Recall that the ecclesiological neutrality of the Toronto statement was emphasized out of consideration for nonmainstream Protestant traditions whose ecclesiologies differed significantly from many member churches of the WCC. From recent conversations, however, we can deduce that perspectives on the relevance and authority of the Toronto statement cannot be clearly organized along denominational lines.

Critics of the Toronto statement have questioned the value of maintaining ecclesiological neutrality in the current ecumenical context. They point out that the *Nature and Mission of the Church* text revealed a great deal of consensus on ecclesiology. Drawing upon studies on the church as *koinonia* as well as on studies on the common apostolic faith, Faith and Order was able to articulate the foundations of an ecumenical ecclesiology, grounded in biblical images and early Christian theology. At the same time, as noted in the previous chapter, I would like to point out that there were multiple areas of disagreement left for the churches to address before moving forward to a consensus statement on the nature and mission of the church. Even if churches agree on the reality of *koinonia*, they may interpret this reality differently, based on their ecclesiological context. For example, the *Nature and Mission of the Church* text highlighted disagreements on the limits of diversity in unity and on the organization of ministry.[24]

In the years following the general assembly in Harare, one can observe two sides forming around the question of whether the Toronto statement is outdated in its pronouncement of ecclesiological neutrality. In his analysis of the responses to the CUV drafting process, Peter Lodberg notes that some churches do not think that the Toronto statement is enough in describing the nature of the council, because "the experiences and the lived fellowship among the churches have gone beyond its description of what the WCC is and is not."[25] This comment is illustrative of

[22] Ibid., 209.

[23] Borovoy, "The Ecclesiological Significance of the WCC," 506.

[24] WCC Commission on Faith and Order, *The Nature and Mission of the Church: A Stage on the Way to a Common Statement* (Geneva: WCC, 2005), 37–39.

[25] Peter Lodberg, "Common Understanding and Vision: An Analysis of the Responses to the Process," *The Ecumenical Review* 50, no. 3 (July 1998): 270.

a common concern raised in response to the Toronto statement. Those who share this interpretation point out that history has provided a better understanding for the nature and purpose of the WCC, so the Toronto statement should be replaced with a more positive pronouncement. Jean-Marie Tillard voices this perspective, stating, "the history of these last fifty years shows that it has an ecclesial density of its own. The time has now come to specify theologically what this is. The letter of the Toronto statement is no longer enough."[26]

At the same time, the Toronto statement continued to be lifted up as a valuable text for addressing the concerns of many Orthodox churches. At a consultation of Orthodox churches on the CUV drafting process, the Toronto statement was affirmed as an important document for encouraging Orthodox participation in the WCC. An Orthodox representative noted, "Our churches participate in the Council with an appreciation of the valuable insights contained in the Toronto Statement of 1950. . . . In accordance with this statement, we view the WCC as a Council of Churches whose primary goal is to assist the member Churches in the quest for the restoration of full communion."[27]

With respect to the divergent views on the value and appropriateness of the Toronto statement for the contemporary discussions on the nature of the WCC, the CUV text did not claim to be a replacement of the Toronto statement. It affirmed the Toronto statement's insight into the nonecclesial status of the WCC, stating:

> The description of the WCC as a "fellowship of churches" indicates clearly that the Council is not itself a church and—as the Toronto statement categorically declares—must never become a "superchurch." Moreover, since the churches within this fellowship themselves maintain different conceptions of the church, their understanding of the significance of this fellowship will also differ. This diversity was present at the WCC's First Assembly in 1948 and at the meeting in 1950 of the WCC's Central Committee in Toronto, which produced the Council's fullest statement of self-definition. It continues to exist after fifty years; indeed, further understandings have emerged as a result of life together.

---

[26] J.-M. R. Tillard, "The World Council of Churches in Quest of Its Identity," *The Ecumenical Review* 50, no. 3 (July 1998): 394.

[27] Final Document of the Inter-Orthodox Consultation on the CUV, Chambesy, 1995, "Common Understanding and Vision of the WCC: Preliminary Observations on the Reflection Process," in Thomas Fitzgerald and Peter Boutenoff, eds., *Turn to God, Rejoice in Hope: Orthodox Reflections on the Way to Harare* (Geneva: WCC, 1998), 56.

Nevertheless, the use of the term "fellowship" in the Basis does suggest that the Council is more than a mere functional association of churches set up to organize activities in areas of common interest.[28]

The discussion on the nature and purpose of the World Council of Churches is still relevant, and the Toronto statement from 1950 still makes its way into conversations. While some argue that the Toronto statement is an outdated document, it is worth noting that it remains one of the most cited texts on the nature of the WCC and the vision of unity that it promotes. Concerns today about inclusive deliberation within the WCC and creating space for broader participation outside of the WCC, I argue, make the insights of the Toronto statement even more relevant than in previous years. Member churches have not achieved the level of consensus and mutual recognition necessary to make the WCC an expression of ecclesial conciliarity, nor have nonmember churches found the WCC to be an expression of the one church of Christ that we seek to make manifest in the ecumenical movement.

Bringing Habermas into the conversation, I would like to point out the importance of having a neutral space for public deliberation prior to articulating a common self-understanding. Recalling his position on the public sphere as a necessary space to negotiate common interests among different perspectives,[29] I suggest that the WCC can function analogously. When the WCC sees itself as a forum for ecumenical dialogue, not adopting the position of a church, it places itself in a unique position to facilitate dialogue across difference. The Toronto statement lays the foundation for the nonecclesial identity of the WCC and, in so doing, provides an important framework for understanding the role of the WCC as a neutral space. I do not mean to suggest that the WCC cannot speak publicly on behalf of the churches. However, the unified voice of the WCC must reflect the positions of each member and not the dominant voice at the expense of inclusivity. This follows Habermas's suggestion that the public sphere should function as an informal space that allows for discourse to occur outside of the level of formal institutions.

In more recent years, the issue of inclusivity has been raised in two specific concerns that relate to the nature and purpose of the WCC.

---

[28] Faith and Order, "Toward a Common Understanding and Vision of the WCC," 107.

[29] For Habermas's discussion of the role of the public sphere in modern democracy, see Jürgen Habermas, *Between Facts and Norms: Contributions to a Discourse Theory of Law and Democracy*, trans. William Rehg (Cambridge, MA: MIT Press, 1996), 183–84.

These are unresolved questions that require a constructive response. The first concern that I will highlight pertains to the decision-making procedures within the council itself. During the preparatory sessions for the general assembly in Harare (1998), the Orthodox churches challenged the WCC to reconsider the appropriateness of parliamentary procedure in its decision making. They advocated for a consensus model of deliberation, which would allow minority voices to be heard in decision-making processes. This conversation raises important questions for consideration in articulating the nature and purpose of the WCC. The second concern deals with the relationships between the WCC and nonmember Christian bodies and/or ecumenical organizations. The growing presence of Pentecostal and Evangelical churches across the globe has challenged the WCC to imagine new ways of fostering Christian unity with churches that do not share many of the underlying assumptions of the WCC. This situation has sparked a contemporary conversation about creating a space for broadened participation in the WCC as one instrument among others within the ecumenical movement.

COMMUNICATION AND CONSENSUS IN THE WCC

Conversations surrounding the nature and mission of the WCC revealed a general consensus that the World Council of Churches was not a council in the sense that the early ecumenical councils of the church were.[30] Because of the real divisions that remain among Christians, the WCC cannot speak with the same authority as an ecumenical council. While many churches understand conciliarity to be a feature of the Christian church and a full manifestation of Christian unity would necessarily include the expression of conciliarity, the churches are still striving for that level of unity that would allow such a manifestation. Within the conversation about the nature and purpose of the WCC, these considerations invite the question, "How can the WCC speak?"

Since its formation, the WCC has faced the challenge of bringing together different ecclesial perspectives and practices into shared life and common witness. It faces the challenge of speaking to this unity that exists without ignoring the divisions that persist. We have seen the way in which the Toronto statement served as a way to prevent the alienation of

---

[30] For the conversation on conciliarity, ecumenical councils, and the World Council of Churches, see Konrad Raiser, "Universal Council, Goal of the Ecumenical Movement?" *Reformed World* 32, no. 5 (March 1971): 202–10.

minority voices from membership in the WCC. It facilitated this through the guarantee that the WCC did not claim to be a superchurch with a presupposed ecclesiology. This prevented the WCC from becoming a forum for mainstream Protestant churches.

The diversity of membership, however, did not eliminate the challenge of speaking of Christian unity in the midst of real divisions. During the preparatory meetings for the general assembly in Harare (1998) and particularly through the conversations about "Toward a Common Understanding and Vision of the World Council of Churches," the Orthodox expressed concerns about the decision-making process employed by the WCC. In an Orthodox reflection on the CUV, an Inter-Orthodox Consultation stated, "Orthodox members of the WCC governing bodies consider themselves a numerical minority. For this reason the WCC is requested to review its constitution with an eye to the distinctive ecclesiological structuring of the Orthodox churches."[31]

Traditionally, the World Council of Churches used a parliamentary procedure of majority vote, placing minority voices at a disadvantage. Parliamentary procedure was used to conduct major WCC meetings and to draft documents. According to the parliamentary procedure, all documents would be created through satisfying the majority of participants in the particular working group. One can see how this process allowed for minority voices to be marginalized and why this is highly problematic in ecumenical dialogue. Churches could be asked to subject serious theological convictions to a voting process and could end up compromising their position to satisfy the perspective of the majority.

In many contexts, particularly in Europe and North America, parliamentary procedure has often been considered to be the best way to ensure fairness in decision-making processes. In the preparation for the general assembly in Harare, it was noted that this understanding of fairness assumes Western biases that work for many European and North American contexts but are not universally appropriate.[32] It is not surprising that the challenge to the majority-vote procedure within the WCC came from the Orthodox churches, who often do not share many of the assumptions of the Christian churches that come out of a Western

---

[31] Inter-Orthodox Consultation on the CUV, Chambesy Switzerland, June 1995, "Common Understanding and Vision of the WCC: Preliminary Observations on the Reflection Process," in Fitzgerald and Bouteneff, eds., *Turn to God, Rejoice in Hope*, 59.

[32] Janice Love, "Doing Democracy Differently: The Special Commission on Orthodox Participation in the WCC," *The Ecumenical Review* 55, no. 1 (January 2003): 73.

tradition.[33] Orthodox participants raised the concern that their voices were being suppressed by the dominant perspective of mainstream Protestantism.[34] While Orthodox churches have been active members in the WCC since the 1960s, they remain a minority voice on many aspects of their theological and cultural perspectives. As noted in the previous chapter, Orthodox churches voiced concerns about the direction of Faith and Order in the years after New Delhi. Orthodox participants cautioned Faith and Order from following the agenda of the world and focusing on social concerns instead of engaging the theological differences that were dividing the churches. They criticized the WCC's growing focus on ethical and social agendas and advocated for a return to what they understood to be the original purpose of the WCC, namely, the promotion of full, visible unity among Christians.[35]

In response to the CUV document, a special commission on Orthodox participation in the WCC raised this issue among others, with the intention of promoting full participation of the Orthodox churches in the WCC. These conversations were motivated by the reality that many Orthodox churches had withdrawn from membership in the council. The special commission stressed the need to reconsider the structure of the WCC to heal this separation and prevent further alienation of Orthodox churches. Their suggestions were guided by the goal of ensuring that the Orthodox experienced themselves on "equal footing" in the WCC. Many Orthodox churches did not experience themselves on equal footing when the agenda of the WCC was directed by "secular concerns" or Western preoccupations. Orthodox commission participant Aram I suggests that "the Council sometimes is used by certain groups to express their own interests. Some churches are pressing certain issues to reach the agenda of the Council. Others feel uncomfortable when these issues are raised, and are not prepared to discuss them."[36] In light of the different understandings of the agenda of the WCC, the Orthodox churches wanted to ensure that their voices would not be marginalized in the discernment

---

[33] See comments on "Orthodox 'culture'" by the Orthodox Task Force 1998, "Orthodox-WCC Relations," in Fitzgerald and Bouthenoff, eds., *Turn to God, Rejoice in Hope*, 177.

[34] "Frequently Asked Questions: The Special Commission on Orthodox Participation in the World Council of Churches," *The Ecumenical Review* 55, no. 1 (January 2003): 43.

[35] "Final Report on the Special Commission on Orthodox Participation in the WCC," *The Ecumenical Review* 55, no.1 (January 2003): 9.

[36] "Report of the Moderator Aram I at the WCC Central Committee Meeting in Geneva 1997," in Fitzgerald and Boutenoff, eds., *Turn to God, Rejoice in Hope*, 121.

of the nature and mission of the WCC. The special commission argued for a rethinking of the decision-making process of the WCC in order to foster equal footing among participants. This meant refraining from decision-making procedures that create a situation of majority-minority.[37]

Many Orthodox churches had already incorporated a consensus model of decision making in the Middle Eastern Council of Churches. During the conversations about the CUV, the ecumenical patriarch present suggested that the consensus model was more in line with Orthodox ecclesiology than the parliamentary procedure traditionally used by the WCC.[38] Using a consensus model promotes dialogue and ongoing discernment among all participants. Ideally, it allows all voices to be heard and prevents coercion and compromise of essential theological understandings. Out of consideration for minority voices, the WCC adopted the consensus model of deliberation at the general assembly in Harare. In his report to the assembly, General Secretary Konrad Raiser promoted the change to the consensus model as one way that the WCC could move forward into the next era of the ecumenical movement, which would require wider participation and a renewed enthusiasm for Christian unity.[39]

One of the motivating factors behind the transition to the consensus model was to create a more harmonious and inclusive ethos in ecumenical dialogue. The special commission addressed this, suggesting that the traditional parliamentary procedure fostered adversarial attitudes rather than cooperation. In their final report, they referred to the traditional WCC decision-making process, stating:

> Proposals are debated "for and against." While amendments are possible—and frequent—speakers are encouraged to argue in favour or against, rather than to explore. On many issues there are of course three or four different viewpoints, not just two. While there is provision for questions concerning any proposals, the adversarial nature of the process is still apparent. In some cultures this adversarial approach, which can even be confrontational, is something to be avoided. Further, it is arguable that the church, being the Body of Christ, is true to its inner nature when it is exploratory, seeking the mind of Christ and striving

---

[37] "Frequently Asked Questions: The Special Commission Report on Orthodox Participation in the WCC," in *The Ecumenical Review* 55, no. 1 (January, 2003): 42–48.

[38] Peter Lodberg, "Common Understanding and Vision: An Analysis of the Responses to the Process," *The Ecumenical Review* 50, no. 3 (July 1998): 274.

[39] Report of the General Secretary Konrad Raiser, in Diane Kessler, ed., *Together on the Way: Official Report of the Eighth Assembly of the WCC* (Geneva: WCC, 1999), 81–102.

after a consensus which can declare: "it seemed good to the Holy Spirit and to us" (Acts 15:28).[40]

This statement certainly confirms my observation at Belem. The process of consensus, though time consuming, encourages a mutual sharing of ideas that goes beyond pragmatic decision making.

The general assembly at Porto Alegre stressed that the consensus process required a spiritual conversion, as indicated in the report of the moderator. Aram I reports that it is necessary to believe in the model of consensus and make the necessary investment in the process. He also stresses the idea that it requires a shift in the general ethos of the WCC.[41] The general assembly offers words of encouragement in response to challenges presented by the consensus model, many of which were foreseen by the special committee. Because the consensus process aims at hearing all voices, it can be lengthy. In a conversation aimed at consensus, there might be fewer decisions or conclusions made. However, the special committee argues that participants are more willing to move the conversation forward when they feel like they have been heard. Consensus, they suggest, does not mean unanimity, and even if a participant does not agree with the majority voice, he or she might be able to enter into consensus if given the opportunity to express a differing perspective. They state, "Because minorities are not 'squashed,' their response is normally to allow the meeting to move ahead to a decision."[42]

It is important to raise the question of whether minority voices are able to move the conversation forward because they feel like they have been heard or whether they are being coerced. This relates directly to the criticism that I received in Belem when I suggested that Habermas's approach to discourse can be applied to the World Council of Churches. The power dynamics that hinder the free exchange of validity claims in actual contexts cannot be ignored in an ecumenical context. In this case, one might question whether minority voices such as the Orthodox churches feel free to participate in the ecumenical conversation even if they are not silenced by process. Habermas's insight into the open-ended process of discourse is helpful here. Consensus, as an ideal,

---

[40] "Final Report of the Special Commission on Orthodox Participation in the WCC," *The Ecumenical Review* 55, no. 1 (January 2003): 27.

[41] Aram I, "Report of the Moderator," *The Ecumenical Review* 58, nos. 1–2 (January–April 2006): 61–62.

[42] "Final Report of the Special Commission on Orthodox Participation in the WCC," *The Ecumenical Review*, 55, no. 1 (January 2003): 33.

serves to regulate conversation, but its achievement does not define the success of the conversation. New insights are always subject to critique and revision; therefore, consensus is never a static reality. At the same time, social groups rely on a level of consensus to stabilize social interaction, so consensus does in fact function despite its always provisional status. Theologically, I argue that ecumenical consensus must always be understood eschatologically. From this perspective, it is always subject to critique and revision in history, as it points to a fullness of unity that is always "not yet" realized. In other words, any consensus that is achieved in an ecumenical context must be understood provisionally because it emerges out of an imperfect communicative encounter.

I find Maria Pia Lara's insights into the critical role of storytelling to be particularly helpful in addressing some of the limitations of Habermas's discourse theory in this particular ecumenical context. As I noted in chapter 1, religious validity claims do not fit neatly into Habermas's framework of rationality. However, they can be understood as rational in the sense that they have the potential to speak critically and intelligibly in multiple contexts and can be defended with good reasons. It is helpful, I suggest, to understand religious validity claims within Pia Lara's understanding of narratives.[43] Theological convictions, or religious validity claims, cannot be legitimated by majority vote, because of their inseparability from the story out of which they emerge. Understanding one's story requires an ongoing conversation, which is promoted in the process of consensus making. As tedious as the process can be, I argue that the WCC's move to a consensus model of deliberation more adequately facilitates the free exchange of religious validity claims than the previous model of parliamentary procedure. Therefore, I think that it is appropriate for the vision of the WCC as it moves into the twenty-first century.

The "Common Understanding and Vision" study was drafted to articulate the ethos of the WCC for the twenty-first century. Observing the changes in the ecumenical landscape within the latter part of the twentieth century, it became clear that the WCC needed to respond to a different context than it did in its formative years. This invited the WCC to rethink its internal relationships, as seen in the conversations around decision making and consensus. Understanding the WCC as an informal public space for discourse is helpful for articulating its role

---

[43] Maria Pia Lara, *Moral Textures: Feminist Narratives in the Public Sphere* (Berkeley: University of California Press, 1999), 2–11.

in the ecumenical movement. Its primary job is not to have member churches vote on binding policies. Its primary job is to provide a space for the promotion of mutual understanding through the development of consensus. Discussions surrounding the CUV also invited the WCC to rethink its external relationships, as seen in the conversations around creating space for broader participation and collaboration with other ecumenical organizations and/or Christian communities that do not share many of the assumptions underlying membership in the WCC.

PARTICIPATION AND COLLABORATION WITH THE WCC

The "Common Understanding and Vision" study also addressed the way in which the WCC should frame its relationships to nonmember churches. This was not a new task for the council, as it has been relating to nonmember churches since its formative years. Perhaps the most notable example of this can be observed in the relationship between the WCC and the Roman Catholic Church. Established in 1965, the Joint Working Group facilitates ongoing collaboration between the WCC and the Roman Catholic Church.[44] While the task was not new, the changing landscape of Christianity and shifts within the ecumenical movement itself presented additional challenges to the WCC to find ways of relating fruitfully to nonmember churches. Specifically, the rise of Pentecostal and Evangelical Christian communities within recent decades has changed the face of global Christianity and has shifted the ecumenical landscape significantly.

While they are too diverse to generalize, many Pentecostal and Evangelical churches have been indifferent or antagonistic toward the ecumenical movement and have chosen not to affiliate with ecumenical organizations such as the WCC.[45] Some fruitful conversations have come out of working groups with Pentecostal and Evangelical churches and the WCC. For example, the World Evangelical Fellowship has participated in WCC meetings since the 1980s.[46] However, by and large, they have avoided membership with the council largely because the goal of visible

---

[44] Thomas Stransky, "Roman Catholic Membership in the World Council of Churches?" *The Ecumenical Review* 20, no. 3 (July 1968): 205–24.

[45] This reflects the assessment of the World Council of Churches as articulated on their website: http://www.oikoumene.org/en/member-churches/church-families/pentecostal-churches.html (accessed December 20, 2009).

[46] George Tsetsis, "The Significance of Regional Ecumenism," in Briggs et al., *History of the Ecumenical Movement*, vol. 3 (Geneva: WCC Publications, 2004), 631.

unity is not theologically relevant for many of the Pentecostal and Evangelical churches or because the language and expression of ecumenism in the WCC does not resonate with their self-understanding.[47]

Some Pentecostal and Evangelical Christians that have participated in the ecumenical movement have articulated the experience of either alienation from the WCC or marginalization within their own churches for their ecumenical commitments. In a letter composed by Evangelical participants at the Sixth General Assembly of the WCC, their theological perspective was raised as a challenge to some of the conclusions of the study "Mission and Evangelism." However, they expressed concern that their challenge was not always heard by the assembly. They stated, "In sum, there were times that we wished that evangelical voices in the churches were given the prominence accorded some theological mavericks."[48] It is important to note that the Evangelical and Pentecostal presence in the ecumenical movement is often looked down upon by their own churches, marginalizing individuals who choose to express their ecumenical commitments. This situation invites the WCC to ask how they can collaborate with such communities in the ecumenical movement without presupposing a common theological basis, such as the one that frames the work of the council. This question motivated conversations on creating space for broader participation with the WCC in the one ecumenical movement.

One of the pressing concerns that emerged within this conversation was the question of how to foster relationships of mutual accountability with nonmember churches. In other words, how can the WCC and nonmember churches act collaboratively instead of competitively with each other in mission, witness, and service? This is especially pertinent with respect to different approaches to evangelization and proselytism. Some members of the WCC voiced concern that the Pentecostal and Evangelical emphasis on growth in numbers poses a problem for many churches within the WCC and creates distrust and animosity among the churches. Different approaches to mission, evangelism, and proselytism are among the primary topics that need to be addressed in order to foster relationships of trust and cooperation between the WCC and Evangelical and Pentecostal Christians.[49]

---

[47] Ibid.

[48] "Evangelicals at Vancouver: An Open Letter," *Mid-Stream* 23, no. 1 (January 1984): 130.

[49] See the report of the second meeting of the Continuation Committee on Ecumenism in the 21st century, January 10–17, Belem, Brazil (33).

Mutual accountability is built into the very concept of the World Council of Churches because it is a fellowship of churches and not simply an institution. Churches participate in the WCC because of a common faith commitment. The ecclesial element of the WCC has been affirmed since the formation of the council, and it is an integral concept in the Toronto statement. At the same time, the WCC is not an ecclesial council in the fullest sense of the term. The fullest embodiment of an ecclesial council is modeled in the early ecumenical councils of the church, which carry more authority because of the unity they manifested. Mary Tanner captures the tension inherent in the nature of a council of churches, acknowledging that the WCC is not a superchurch, using the words of the Toronto statement but also highlighting the implications of being a fellowship of churches. She states:

> Nevertheless it is as churches together are helped to name and claim what *already* exists in their belonging to one another in the fellowship, that they are given the confidence to face the challenges posed by those things that continue to divide them and the courage to go on working for visible unity.[50]

To echo the perspective of Visser 't Hooft among others, the WCC is understood to be a provisional entity and necessarily has institutional qualities. The challenge presented here is to integrate the institutional elements and the ecclesial reality of the WCC into a common understanding and meaningful vision.

During the preparation of the CUV, the institutional quality of the WCC was debated. There was a concern that the institutional quality of the WCC was being emphasized over the ecclesial reality of it.[51] Discussions about decision-making processes and the institutional profile of the WCC could give the impression that the WCC was more like a nonecclesial organization than a fellowship of churches. Visser 't Hooft took up this question years prior to the CUV study. He suggested that the WCC had become institutionalized but that this was an inevitable process. The warning against the overinstitutionalization of churches and ecumenical councils was merited, he suggested. At the same time, rejecting all institutions as bad is simply impractical since churches and fellowships

---

[50] Mary Tanner, "Towards a Common Understanding and Vision: A Faith and Order Perspective," *The Ecumenical Review* 50, no. 3 (July 1998): 362.

[51] Konrad Raiser, "Report of the General Secretary," in Diane Kessler, ed., *Together on the Way*, 94–98.

of churches need to live and act in the world. The institutional quality of the WCC developed to facilitate its job of promoting Christian unity, and this provisional function requires an institutional embodiment. [52]

Michael Root describes the relationship between the ecclesial and institutional reality of the WCC with the concept of "ecclesial density." He uses the notion of ecclesial density to point to the reality that councils, communions, and churches have different levels of ecclesial unity, which enables them to speak and act as churches. He notes that Christian World Communions have a deeper level of ecclesial density, which enables them to speak with more authority than the WCC.[53] This is a helpful way to think about the possibility of church being present but not fully manifested within a particular organization. It is also helpful in allowing us to reframe church and institutionalization in a way that is not totally in opposition. As Visser 't Hooft notes, institutions are not entirely bad and they do serve a purpose. Institutions become paralyzing to churches when they are not kept in balance with the ecclesial density of the organization.

This debate is significant for discernment on the nature and purpose of the WCC within the ecumenical movement. Since the WCC is not the full embodiment of the unity we seek, it cannot exhaust the reality of the ecumenical movement. The institutional quality of the WCC exists provisionally for the service of the one church of Christ that we seek to make manifest. The ecclesial reality that the WCC embodies as a fellowship of churches, which must be recognized alongside the institutional aspect, is made manifest through the WCC. However, it is not created by the WCC or possessed by the WCC. It can only be manifested because it already exists among the churches themselves. This reminds us of the fact that there is one ecumenical movement, grounded in the unity in which Christ grounds us and in the greater unity to which Christ calls us. The WCC participates in this one ecumenical movement but does not create or possess this movement. This generally accepted stance invites the WCC to look for ways of collaborating with nonmember churches in the ecumenical movement.

This perspective motivated the development of the Global Christian Forum. Conversations about the formation of an organization that could

---

[52] Willem A. Visser 't Hooft, "Is the Ecumenical Movement Suffering from Institutional Paralysis?" *The Ecumenical Review* 25, no. 3 (July 1973): 295–310.

[53] Michael Root, "Christian World Communions and the CUV Process," *The Ecumenical Review* 50, no. 3 (July 1998): 330–37.

facilitate ecumenical dialogue among churches that were not members of the WCC began in a particular way at Harare (1998). These conversations related to the WCC's interest in creating a space for wider participation and collaboration among nonmember churches. The Global Christian Forum is autonomous from the WCC but collaborates with it in promoting Christian unity. At their first meeting in Nairobi in 2007, the Global Christian Forum articulated its guiding purpose statement as follows:

> To create an open space wherein representatives from a broad range of Christian churches and interchurch organizations, which confess the triune God and Jesus Christ as perfect in His divinity and humanity, can gather to foster mutual respect, to explore and address together common challenges.[54]

The implications of the Global Christian Forum and the efforts of the WCC to broaden their participation in the ecumenical movement are still to be grasped. Without a doubt, it is reflective of a shift in the ecumenical movement, within which the WCC needs to locate itself as one instrument among others. The CUV is still in the reception process of the WCC. Coupled with the emphasis on ecclesiology, the nature of visible unity and the nature of the council and its role within the ecumenical movement are still debated among the churches. As we look for a consensus on these important topics, we have to address some important questions. How can we understand, in a positive sense, the institutional quality of the WCC? How does the institutional aspect of the WCC relate to the ecclesial reality of the fellowship of churches that compose it? How can we locate the WCC within the broader context of the ecumenical movement in such a way that neither diminishes its value nor ignores other expressions of ecumenical commitment? In the next section, I will address these questions by drawing upon a critical appropriation of Habermas's theory of discourse and the roles of institutions and the public sphere in modern societies.

THE WCC AS A FORUM FOR ECUMENICAL DIALOGUE

While Habermas does not provide an analysis of the World Council of Churches, he does offer an extensive theory of modern institutions that is helpful for addressing the questions raised in this chapter. One of

---

[54] Global Christian Forum's website, http://www.globalchristianforum.org/document/article.php?no=4 (accessed April 9, 2009).

the reemerging concerns in the discussions surrounding the CUV is the institutionalization of the WCC and what this means for the WCC as a fellowship of churches. Years prior to the development of the CUV, Visser 't Hooft expressed ambivalence about the institutional quality of the WCC. In many ways, Habermas, in his critical social theory, echoes this ambivalence toward modern institutions. Like Visser 't Hooft's perspective on the WCC, Habermas understands the development of institutions to be an inevitable result of modernization, but he cautions against the overinstitutionalization of social organizations at the risk of replacing the social integration of the lifeworld with the once-removed system integration of the institution. In this section, I critically apply Habermas's social theory to the questions surrounding the nature and purpose of the World Council of Churches with particular attention to the issues raised in the first part of this chapter. First, I explore the shift toward a consensus model of decision making within the WCC, using Habermas's discourse theory. Then, I analyze the conversations around creating space for broader participation with the WCC, using Habermas's theory of society as consisting of both systems and lifeworlds. Finally, I revisit the conversations on the Toronto statement, using Habermas's insights to argue for its value in contemporary conversations about the nature and purpose of the WCC.

As a critical theorist, Habermas is concerned with the transformation of modern society through an emancipatory use of reason. His vision of an emancipated society is one that allows for social coordination through consensus achieved through dominance-free discourse. This discourse is made possible through the rational structure of language use. Recall that Habermas develops a discourse theory that postulates that consensus serves as a regulatory principle for the process of reaching understanding through agreement.[55] Since discourse always occurs in real situations that complicate the use of reason, the ideal of consensus is rarely achieved and all shared understanding is itself open to change through ongoing discourse. The goal of consensus requires a commitment to the process of discourse and a willingness to subject one's validity claims to the hearer's acceptance or rejection. When the goal of consensus is displaced by a strategic aim of one of the communicators, the process of discourse can become irrational, manipulative, and exclusionary.[56]

---

[55] Jürgen Habermas, "Richard Rorty's Pragmatic Turn," in Maeve Cooke, ed., *On the Pragmatics of Communication* (Cambridge, MA: MIT Press, 1998), 365–77.

[56] Habermas, "Actions, Speech Acts, Linguistically Mediated Interactions, and Lifeworld," in Cooke, ed., *On the Pragmatics of Communication*, 220–27.

Returning to the context of the World Council of Churches, I argue that Habermas's insights are helpful. The shift toward a consensus model of decision making was grounded in the experience of some churches who felt like they were repeatedly asked to compromise their positions in favor of the majority preference. The Orthodox churches pointed out the inadequacies of the parliamentary process of decision making as they articulated the experience of being silenced or asked to compromise to the agenda of the majority. Recalling insights gleaned from a critical analysis of the Council of Florence, unity is not achieved through coercion or by compromising the integrity of one's ecclesial identity. Unity can only be established through an ongoing exchange of narrative self-understandings.

One of the challenges to the consensus model of decision making is that it is, for all practical purposes, difficult to implement. It requires a commitment to listening to all perspectives and talking through all objections. Consensus, as noted by Konrad Raiser, requires a shift in ethos.[57] In other words, it necessitates not only a change in process but also a change in attitude. It invites participants to enter into the process intentionally and prayerfully with a commitment to inclusive and dominance-free dialogue. The ideal of consensus, even when it is not fully reached, influences the process of dialogue and changes the way people approach the conversation. This situation gives evidence to the assertion that the goal itself shapes how participants approach dialogue.

Does the consensus model achieve the objective of inclusive and dominance-free communication? Critics of Habermas's theory point out that the ideal of consensus is limited in its counterfactual nature. Recalling Benhabib's suggestion that the ideal of abstract universality is not achievable or helpful invites us to consider the limitations of the principle of consensus in real-life situations.[58] Habermas's understanding of consensus assumes a strong model of reason. While his approach to reason is multidimensional and intersubjective, critics have suggested that Habermas's emphasis on reason downplays the role and legitimacy of other forms of knowledge in social coordination and communication.

This critique is relevant in the context of the WCC. Recalling my experience in Belem, the objection was rightfully raised that the consensus

---

[57] Konrad Raiser, "Report of General Secretary," in Diane Kessler, ed., *Together on the Way*, 94–102.

[58] Seyla Benhabib, *Situating the Self: Gender, Community and Postmodernism in Contemporary Ethics* (New York: Routledge, 1992), 26–38.

model of deliberation is just as reliant on the Western rational tradition as the parliamentary model is. The WCC, as a fellowship of churches from all over the globe, has continually searched for ways to avoid privileging a dominant Western framework, allowing non-Western voices to be heard. Paradoxically, the shift to the consensus model in the WCC was motivated by the intention to avoid Western cultural hegemony. However, reliance on the consensus model, with its privileging of rationality, can itself be understood as an assertion of Western advantage. Some argue that the consensus model is inadequate in light of the cultural diversity of the WCC.

In response to this objection, Maria Pia Lara's critique of Habermas is particularly relevant. She suggests that Habermas's theory of knowledge can be more inclusive through an expanded understanding of rationality. Recall that she invites us to consider Habermas's earlier work on the public sphere, which, combined with Hannah Arendt's insights into the transformative role of storytelling, offers a broader understanding of rationality. Maintaining a commitment to critical theory, Lara suggests that emancipatory reason is not abstract and disembodied but grounded in private lifeworld realities that can be expressed through narrative.[59] While this critique does not resolve all of the inadequacies of Habermas's theory with respect to the context of the WCC, it does open up greater possibilities for including non-Western approaches in the implementation of the consensus process. We can expect such approaches to provide important critiques and revisions of the consensus model that Habermas and Habermasian thinkers may overlook.

One must acknowledge the limitations of any attempt to create non-coercive conversation in a context that has been shaped by a history of power imbalances. Spivak's postcolonial insights serve as a reminder of the importance of acknowledging the historical/contextual trajectory of one's theory. Habermas's theory of communicative action is grounded in the Western rationalist tradition, which will not provide a perfect model for the multicultural community of the WCC. At the same time, as Spivak reminds us, one should not disregard a theory because of its limitations; theorists must locate themselves and acknowledge the limitations of the theory.[60] Allowing Habermas's insights to inform and critique the

---

[59] Lara, *Moral Textures*, 12–18.
[60] Spivak does not disregard the value of feminist theory. In her essay "Can the Subaltern Speak?" she critiques the practice of theorists denying their representational privilege but does not suggest that theory is not important. See Spivak, "Can the Subaltern

emerging consensus procedures of the WCC will be helpful in evaluating its appropriateness. In addition, the use of consensus within the real-life context of the WCC will provide insights that can be used to inform and critique the theory.

Habermas's theory is also helpful in addressing the other key question that emerged out of the discussion of the nature and purpose of the WCC, namely, how the WCC can best operate as an institution that is also a fellowship of churches. Habermas's social theory implicitly addresses this question. Recall that Habermas describes modern societies from both an internalist perspective and an externalist perspective, identifying them as both lifeworlds and systems.[61] Exploring the interaction between systems and lifeworlds, Habermas articulates an ambivalent attitude toward modern institutions. The rationalization of the lifeworld necessitates systemic support to maintain social cohesion. Institutions, in this sense, are an inevitable result of rationalization and not necessarily the embodiment of technical interests alone. In other words, they can operate according to the interests of the lifeworld. However, modern social pathologies develop when systems colonize the lifeworld in the sense that they are no longer subordinate to lifeworld interests but rather shape those interests.[62]

The World Council of Churches, as an institution, can benefit from Habermas's insights on this process. Concerns about the institutionalization of the WCC are grounded in the fear that the institutional nature will be emphasized over the reality of the WCC as a fellowship of churches. Recall the Toronto statement's insistence that the WCC as an organization derives its authority from the churches that participate in it. If we focus on the institutional reality of the WCC and overlook the churches themselves, there is a risk of subordinating the authority of the churches to the agenda of an organization. This is contrary to the purpose of the WCC, which is to facilitate Christian unity by bringing churches together. It is not meant to create unity or negotiate church unions.

The type of social integration that is experienced in a church can be likened to the social integration of the lifeworld. The lifeworld provides

---

Speak?" in Patrick Williams and Laura Chrisman, eds., *Colonial Discourse and Post-Colonial Theory: A Reader* (New York: Columbia University Press, 1994), 91–92.

[61] Jürgen Habermas, *The Theory of Communicative Action*, vol. 2, *Lifeworld and System: A Critique of Functionalist Reason*, trans. Thomas McCarthy (Boston: Beacon Press, 1987), 118.

[62] Ibid., 153–55.

an immediate social integration through a shared framework of interests, beliefs, and taken-for-granted knowledge. It is grounded in an inherited tradition that facilitates common assumptions and experiences. Its authority is legitimated by the participants in the tradition, for whom it is rational. It is considered rational in the sense that participants affirm the validity of the truth claims raised. The kind of social integration experienced on the level of the World Council of Churches is different. The WCC does not assume the authority of a church because it cannot assume the commonality experienced by participants in a shared tradition. The WCC has to make its truth claims explicit and subject them to ongoing discourse in order to be validated by its participants. The social cohesion experienced on the level of the WCC has the potential of becoming like the social cohesion generated by modern institutions, which maintain a bureaucratic element. Systems cannot rely on taken-for-granted knowledge; rather, they gain their authority from the recognition of their explicit truth claims for the community that they serve.

How does the analogy of lifeworlds/churches and institutions/WCC help in the conversation about the nature and function of the WCC? For one thing, it provides theoretical reasoning for the assertion that the WCC is to be informed by the lives of the churches. As a fellowship of churches, the WCC exists to manifest the will of the churches and to facilitate interaction of the churches. Habermas reminds us that systems emerge out of and should remain informed by the immediate reality of the lifeworld. Problems occur when systems become divorced from and more powerful than the lifeworld. Similarly, critics have responded to the institutionalization of the WCC with concerns that it can become too focused on organizational concerns and forget that it is grounded in the churches that participate in it. Using Habermas's notion of the public sphere, I would like to point out the need for an informal space that exists prior to formal institutions in the context of ecumenical dialogue. The WCC can serve this function as long as it remains informed by the churches themselves and avoids overinstitutionalization by acting like a public sphere, or an informal forum for discourse.

With respect to the efforts to create a space for wider participation with the WCC, it is again important to emphasize the functional reality of the WCC. Since the churches always exist prior to the WCC, the council should see itself as a means to church unity and not as an end in itself. Highlighting the authority of the churches over the council promotes an understanding of the council as one vehicle among others in the work of the ecumenical movement. The existence of the Global Christian Forum is helpful in framing the role of the WCC within the context of the one ecumenical movement. Institutions do not exist for their own end but should remain open to revision that is informed by the experiences of those who participate in them.

During the discussions surrounding the CUV, the contemporary appropriateness of the Toronto statement was questioned. Recall that critics of the Toronto statement argued that it said too little about what the WCC actually is, focusing on what the WCC is not. They argued that we need a positive statement about the WCC instead of emphasizing the neutrality and open-ended ecclesiological position of the council. These critics pointed out that the history of the WCC has provided a more solid framework for articulating an ecumenical ecclesiology and a common vision of unity. At the same time, it is important to note recent developments in the ecumenical movement that remind us of the real diversity that exists among Christian churches. The Orthodox churches reminded us that minority voices are silenced when the majority controls the agenda of ecumenical dialogue. The growing presence of Pentecostal and Evangelical churches reminds us that a large number of the world's Christians do not share the vision of the World Council of Churches, requiring a reimagining of the role of the council in the ecumenical movement.

I argue that the insights of the Toronto statement are still important in today's ecumenical climate. With a diversity of ecclesiologies and approaches to unity, the Toronto statement provides a reminder that the WCC should be an inclusive and open space for churches to encounter each other. Drawing upon Habermas's insights on the relationship between lifeworld and systems, I argue that the institution of the WCC should remain subordinate to the lives of the churches. While these lives are diverse, they can also be shared. This sharing requires a space that facilitates honesty, openness, mutual accountability, and the possibility of transformation. The WCC remains an important instrument in this endeavor; however, an important instrument can never replace the one who operates it. The churches themselves are the lifeblood of the ecumenical movement, so the nature and purpose of the WCC should always be informed by them.

My proposed approach to ecumenical dialogue invites us to understand Christian unity eschatologically. The consensus that we achieve and embody in ecumenical institutions is always provisional, open to new insights as we come to understand the fullness of the church. Habermas's perspective disrupts any attempt to define the end goal of the ecumenical movement and reminds us that the reality of the church, the *Una Sancta* that we believe in, cannot be reduced to human efforts. Habermas invites us to see unity in the process of reaching consensus and frees us to acknowledge the real diversities that still exist. This understanding can renew a commitment to the ecumenical movement without ignoring the ambiguity on the nature of the church and the nonlinear process of arriving at unity. Recalling Letty Russell's eschatological ecclesiology is helpful here. Her image of the Church in the Round, a place of inclusivity and equality, is particularly relevant in contemporary conversations on decision-making processes and broadening participation in the WCC. She reminds us that this metaphor for the church should always issue a challenge to the church that we experience in history. She states, "The church is a sign of the coming fulfillment of God's promise for New Creation. As a sign, it is always provisional and is in constant need of renewal in order to make an authentic witness to God's love and justice in changing historical, political, economic, and social contexts."[63]

---

[63] Letty Russell, *Church in the Round: Feminist Interpretation of the Church* (Louisville: Westminster John Knox Press, 1993), 13–14.

Conclusion

The ecumenical movement in the twenty-first century may look like the WCC's Belem meeting writ large. The procedure of consensus constantly displaces the goal of the conversation. As different voices emerge, the topic of conversation shifts. When we are no longer voting yes or no on a presupposed objective, we create the possibility for unexpected insights. When individuals can express their truths without pressure to conform to the objective of the dialogue, self-revealing narratives are welcomed to the table. Mutual understanding occurs as a process of ongoing encounters with the other. Within this context, I contend that individuals and churches should not have to choose between either retaining their particularity or realizing greater unity. The process of coming to mutual understanding creates unity within the diversity. In other words, unity is realized in the process even if it is not realized in an end goal.

The unity that we seek in the ecumenical movement may not look like the unity that the first generation of ecumenists had imagined. In other words, we may never realize in history the organic unity imagined by the Third General Assembly at New Delhi. Recall the WCC's optimistic vision in 1963:

> We believe that the unity which is both God's will and his gift to his Church is being made visible as all in each place who are baptized into Jesus Christ and confess him as Lord and Savior are brought by the Holy Spirit into one fully committed fellowship, holding the one apostolic faith, preaching one Gospel, breaking one bread, joining in common prayer, and having a corporate life reaching out in witness and service to all and who at the same time are united with the whole Christian fellowship in all places and all ages in such wise that ministry and members are accepted by all, and that all can act and speak together as occasion requires for the tasks to which God calls his people.[1]

[1] Third General Assembly of the World Council of Churches at New Delhi, "Report of the Section on Unity," in Lukas Vischer, ed., *A Documentary History of the Faith and Order Movement 1927–1963* (St. Louis, MO: Bethany Press, 1963), 145.

While New Delhi's vision of unity seems wonderful and worthy of pursuit, it is not clear how all churches fit into that vision. What does shared ministry look like for Episcopalians and Quakers? What does a common breaking of the bread mean for Orthodox Christians and Lutherans? The answers to these questions are by no means obvious. The ambiguity of such questions stresses the point that mutual understanding must precede every other ecumenical goal. The ecclesial self-understandings of Christians around the world are diverse, requiring an ongoing process of listening to each other, discovering together what a common vision of the church might look like.

At the same time, if we consider this vision eschatologically, locating the nature of the unity we seek within the ultimate mystery of the church we believe in, we still have reason to invest ourselves in the ecumenical movement. The Second Vatican Council's insistence upon the pilgrim status of the Christian community on earth reinforces the eschatological quality of the ecumenical movement. *Lumen Gentium* states, "For if we continue to love one another and to join in praising the Most Holy Trinity—all of us who are sons of God and form one family in Christ—we will be faithful to the deepest vocation of the Church and will share in a foretaste of the liturgy of perfect glory" (LG 51). With this in mind we are invited to consider that the worth of the ecumenical journey is inherent in the eschatological dimension of Christian existence and is not measured by our own achievements. We have reason to labor for the ecumenical movement even if we cannot yet break bread together. We have reason to look back upon the century of ecumenical work and celebrate the unity we have realized, even if our ministers do not as yet speak in common. "For if continue to love one another" (LG 51), we are on the right track. If anything can rekindle enthusiasm for the ecumenical movement in the twenty-first century, I think it lies in this eschatological vision.

In this book, I have proposed an approach to unity that sustains dialogue within this eschatological reality. Drawing upon Habermas's distinction between strategic and communicative action, I critiqued the precipitous attempts to define the goal of ecumenical dialogue within a particular ecclesiological framework. If we are to avoid strategic ecumenical encounters as observed in Zeno's *Henoticon* and the Council of Florence, we must first seek to understand the other and allow every other goal to emerge out of that basic understanding. Strategic ecumenism, which might involve bargaining, manipulation, or an unwillingness to hear the truth of the other, damages the Christian community. The history of ecumenism is full of subtle and not-so-subtle strategic actions that offer ecumenical lessons for today. The story of the Council of Florence still matters because it is woven into the narrative that shapes the ecclesial self-understandings of the Eastern churches.

Because narratives matter in a communicative encounter and because the way that we imagine consensus is always shaped by actual discourse, measuring the success of ecumenical dialogue is more complicated than Habermas's theory tends to allow. How do we know when we have achieved mutual understanding—or, in Habermas's language, rational agreement on validity claims—in an ecumenical context? This is a difficult question because ecclesial identities are constantly shifting. As churches respond to the signs of the times, bringing their traditions into dialogue with an ever-changing world, their self-understandings develop. Religious discourse, I argue, is unique in that it aims to articulate universally applicable truths out of a contextually bound narrative. Using Maria Pia Lara's insights on the public role of narrative to supplement Habermas's discourse theory, I argue that religious validity claims are rational in the sense that they can be intelligible outside of the community of believers that articulates them. However, coming to understand someone's narrative involves a long process of dialogue without a clear end goal. This reality complicates Habermas's understanding of consensus as a regulatory principle for discourse. Consensus cannot be imagined as a disembodied or abstract ideal. As Seyla Benhabib points out, consensus is always being informed by the actual relationships that develop in the dialogue. Therefore, consensus as a goal is always in flux, being realized and then disrupted in the communicative encounter.

The kind of ongoing dialogue that is required for Christians to come to understand each other necessitates a particular forum. I suggest that the World Council of Churches has the potential for serving as a forum for ongoing ecumenical dialogue as long as it remains informed by the dynamic traditions that compose it. Habermas's insight into the relationship between lifeworlds and systems informs my argument that the WCC as an institution should be subordinate to the lived truths of the churches that legitimate its existence. This insight helps to locate the WCC within the larger ecumenical movement that is motivated by churches that do not participate directly with the WCC. Highlighting the ecclesial neutrality of the WCC stresses that it is an organization that serves to promote the desire for unity that emerges from the churches themselves.

The World Council of Churches acting a forum for ecumenical dialogue can serve as a model for the negotiation of religious identity across difference, which has implications beyond the ecumenical movement. In chapter 1, I highlighted Habermas's interest in the public role of religion in a secular context. I support Habermas's insistence upon the need for an informal public space where religious and secular individuals can come together to address social, political, and ethical questions. His proposal, however, leaves me wondering how a common language will emerge from this encounter that will truly take into account the particular contributions of religious thinkers. If secular language is assumed to be the more generally accessible language that will ultimately be used to formulate public policy, how can we ensure that religious voices are heard?

Understanding the WCC as a model is helpful in addressing this question. By incorporating the consensus model of deliberation into its decision-making processes, the WCC manifests the potential of achieving unity through ongoing discourse. The open-ended quality of the consensus model promotes mutual understanding through the exchange of religious narratives. These narratives, using Lara's insights, have a rational, critical quality because they can reframe relationships in a public space. In other words, when narratives come into contact with each other, transformation should be expected. Out of this space, a new language may emerge. In an ecumenical context, the new language should be one that more adequately expresses the unity to which Christians are called. The WCC should then reflect the language of unity that is discovered in the process of ongoing dialogue. In effect, it models how norms can develop out of a pluralistic context in such a way that honors the particularity of each narrative.

Christian *koinonia* can be a prophetic witness to diversity in unity within our globalized context. An approach to community that promotes a dynamic sense of belonging without squashing the particularity of one's identity is needed in a context marked by ambiguity and anxiety. Modeling the commitment to the process of consensus, knowing how tedious the process can be, is prophetic within a globalized world characterized by a plurality of options for defining oneself and relating to others. Ultimately, I think that this commitment, which the ecumenical movement can foster, allows the Christian community to promote global solidarity by manifesting a sustainable model of unity.

Bibliography

Baugher, N. J. "Unity Needs to be Visible." *Brethren Life and Thought* 3 (1958): 10–16.

Bauman, Zygmunt. *Globalization: The Human Consequences.* Cambridge: Polity Press, 1998.

Beffa, Pierre, ed. *Index to the World Council of Churches' Official Statements and Reports 1948–1994.* Geneva: WCC, 1995.

Bellah, Robert, et al. *Habits of the Heart: Individualism and Commitment in American Life.* 3rd ed. Berkeley: University of California Press, 2007.

Benedict XVI. *Caritas in Veritate.* English translation by the United States Conference of Catholic Bishops. Washington, DC: United States Conference of Catholic Bishops, 2009.

Benhabib, Seyla. *Situating the Self.* New York: Routledge, 1992.

Benhabib, Seyla, and Fred Dallmayr, eds. *The Communicative Ethics Controversy.* Cambridge, MA: MIT Press, 1990.

Best, Thomas, ed. *Beyond Unity-in-Tension: Unity, Renewal and the Community of Women and Men.* Geneva: WCC, 1988.

———. *Living Today towards Visible Unity: The Fifth International Consultation of United and Uniting Churches.* Geneva: WCC, 1988.

———. *Vancouver to Canberra, 1983–1990: Report of the Central Committee of the World Council of Churches to the Seventh Assembly.* Geneva: WCC, 1990.

Best, Thomas, and Theodore J. Nottingham, eds. *The Vision of Christian Unity: A Life Given to the Ecumenical Quest: Essays in Honor of Paul A. Crow, Jr.* Indianapolis: Oikoumene Publications, 1997.

Bilheimer, Robert. *Breakthrough: The Emergence of the Ecumenical Tradition.* Geneva: WCC, 1989.

Birmelé, André, ed. *Local Ecumenism: How Church Unity is Seen and Practiced by Congregations.* Geneva: WCC, 1984.

Bohman, James. *Public Deliberation: Pluralism, Complexity, and Democracy.* Cambridge, MA: MIT Press, 1996.

———. "Theories, Practices, and Pluralism: A Pragmatic Interpretation of Critical Social Science." *Philosophy of the Social Sciences* 28 (1999): 459–80.

Borovoy, Vitaly. "The Ecclesiological Significance of the WCC: The Legacy and Promise of Toronto." *The Ecumenical Review* 40, nos. 3–4 (July–October 1988): 504–18.

Brand, Arie. *The Force of Reason: An Introduction to Habermas' Theory of Communicative Action*. Boston: Allen & Unwin, 1990.

Bria, Ion, ed. *The Sense of Ecumenical Tradition: The Ecumenical Witness and Vision of the Orthodox*. Geneva: WCC, 1991.

Briggs, John, Mercy Amba Oduyoye, and Georges Tsetsis, eds. *A History of the Ecumenical Movement*. Vol. 3. Geneva: WCC, 2004.

Browning, Don, and Francis Schussler Fiorenza, eds. *Habermas, Modernity and Public Theology*. New York: Crossroads, 1992.

Caird, George Bradford. *Making it Visible*. London: British Council of Churches, 1964.

Churches Council for Covenanting. *Towards Visible Unity: Proposals for a Covenant; The Report of the Churches Council for Covenanting*. London: Churches Council for Covenanting, 1980.

———. *On Behalf of the Covenant: A Statement by Six Anglican Members on Behalf of the Report of the Churches' Council for Covenanting Entitled "Towards Visible Unity: Proposals for a Covenant."* London: CIO Publishing, 1978.

The Church of England Board for Mission and Unity. *Anglicans in Dialogue: The Contribution of Theological Dialogues to the Search for the Visible Unity of the Churches in the 1980s*. London: General Synod of the Church of England, Board for Mission and Unity, 1984.

———. *The Meissen Common Statement: On the Way to Visible Unity; A Report by the House of Bishops*. London: Church of England, 1990.

———. *Visible Unity: Ten Propositions*. London: Churches' Unity Commission, 1976.

———. *Visible Unity in Life and Mission: 2nd Report*. London: Church Information Office, 1976.

———. *Visible Unity in Life and Mission: The Ten Propositions; A Discussion Paper for the Church of England*. London: Church Information Office, 1978.

Cooke, Maeve. "Salvaging and Secularizing the Semantic Contents of Religion: The Limitations of Habermas' Postmetaphysical Proposal." *The International Journal of Philosophy and Religion* 60 (2006): 187–207.

Cope, Brian, and Michael Kinnamon, eds. *The Ecumenical Movement: An Anthology of Key Texts and Voices*. Grand Rapids, MI: Eerdmans, 1997.

Council of Florence. *Laetentur Coeli: The Decree for the Greeks*. Translated by Henry Denzinger. *The Sources of Catholic Dogma*. Fitzwilliam, NH: Loreto Publications, 2001.

Craig, Clarence. "The Reality of the Church and Our Doctrines about the Church." *The Ecumenical Review* 3, no. 3 (April 1951): 213–66.

Crow, Paul A., Jr. "Ecumenics as Reflections on Models of Christian Unity." *The Ecumenical Review* 39, no. 4, (October 1987): 389–403.

Cullmann, Oscar. *Unity through Diversity: Its Foundation, and a Contribution to the Discussion Concerning the Possibilities of Its Actualization.* Philadelphia: Fortress Press, 1988.

Deschner, John. "Visible Unity as Conciliar Fellowship: Meeting in Jerusalem Reported in Acts 15 and Galatians 2." *The Ecumenical Review* 28, no. 1 (1976): 22–27.

Dillistone, F. W. "Church Union: Organic or Federal?" *Theology Today* 5 (1948): 186–98.

Dumont, C. J. *Approaches to Christian Unity: Doctrine and Prayer.* Translated with an introduction by Henry St. John. London: Darton, Longman and Todd, 1959.

Duquoc, Christian. *Provisional Churches: An Essay in Ecumenical Ecclesiology.* London: SCM Press, 1986.

Fahey, Michael, ed. *Ecumenism: A Bibliographical Overview.* Westport, CT: Greenwood, 1992.

Fey, Harold E. *A History of the Ecumenical Movement: The Ecumenical Advance 1948–1968.* 2nd ed. Geneva: WCC, 1986.

Flannery, Austin, ed. *Vatican Council II.* Vol. 1, *The Conciliar and Post Conciliar Documents.* New revised edition. Northport, NY: Costello Publishing, 1996.

Frend, W. C. H. *The Rise of Christianity.* Philadelphia: Fortress Press, 1984.

Fries, Heinrich, and Karl Rahner. *Unity of the Churches: An Actual Possibility.* Philadelphia: Fortress Press, 1985.

Fulton, C. D. "Organic Church Union: Are Churchmen Ready?" *Christianity Today* 10 (November 5, 1965): 5.

Gaddis, Michael, and Richard Price. *The Acts of the Council of Chalcedon.* 3 Vols. Liverpool: Liverpool University Press, 2005.

Gassmann, Günther, ed. *Documentary History of Faith and Order, 1963–1993.* Geneva: WCC, 1993.

Geday, Michel. *Oecuménisme et Eglise Visible.* Chevetogne: Ed. de Chevetogne, 1963.

Gennadios of Sassima, ed. *Grace in Abundance: Orthodox Reflections on the Way to Porto Alegre.* Geneva: WCC, 2005.

Gill, David Muir, ed. *The Gathered Life: Official Report, Sixth Assembly World Council of Churches, Vancouver, Canada 24 July–10 August 1983.* Geneva: WCC, 1983.

Gill, Joseph. *The Council of Florence.* Cambridge: Cambridge University Press, 1959.

———. *Personalities of the Council of Florence.* Oxford: Basil/Blackwell, 1964.

Goodall, Norman, ed. *The Uppsala Report 1968: Official Report of the Fourth Assembly of the World Council of Churches Uppsala, July 4–20 1968.* Geneva: WCC, 1968.

Goosen, Gideon. *Bringing Churches Together: A Popular Introduction to Ecumenism.* Geneva: WCC, 2001.

Gottschalk-Mazouz, Niels. *Diskursethik.* Berlin: Akademie, 2000.

Gros, Jeffrey, ed. *The Search for Visible Unity: Baptism, Eucharist, Ministry.* Geneva: WCC, 1984.

Gros, Jeffrey, Eamon McManus, and Ann Riggs, *Introduction to Ecumenism.* New York: Paulist Press, 1998.

Gros, Jeffrey, Harding Meyer, and William Rusch, eds. *Growth in Agreement II: Reports and Agreed Statements of Ecumenical Conversations at a World Level, 1982–1998.* Geneva: WCC, 2000.

Gros, Jeffrey, and William Rusch, eds. *Deepening Communion: International Ecumenical Documents with Roman Catholic Participation.* Washington, DC: United States Catholic Conference, 1998.

Groupe des Dombes. *Pour la Conversion des Églises.* Geneva: WCC, 1993.

Günther, Klaus. *The Sense of Appropriateness.* Translated by J. Farrell. Albany: SUNY Press, 1993.

Habermas, Jürgen. *Between Facts and Norms: Contributions to a Discourse Theory of Law and Democracy.* Translated by William Rehg. Cambridge, MA: MIT Press, 1996.

———. *Between Naturalism and Religion.* Translated by C. Cronin. Cambridge: Polity Press, 2008.

———. *Communication and the Evolution of Society.* Translated by Thomas McCarthy. Boston: Beacon Press, 1979.

———. *The Divided West.* Translated by C. Cronin. Cambridge: Polity Press, 2006.

———. *The Future of Human Nature.* Translated by W. Rehg, M. Pensky, and H. Beister. Cambridge: Polity Press, 2003.

———. *Inclusion of the Other: Studies in Political Theory.* Edited by C. Cronin and P. DeGreiff. Cambridge, MA: MIT Press, 1998.

———. "Justice and Solidarity: On the Discussion Concerning Stage 6." Translated by S. W. Nicholsen. In *The Moral Domain,* edited by T. E. Wren, 224–51. Cambridge, MA: MIT Press, 1990.

———. *Justification and Application: Remarks on Discourse Ethics.* Translated by Ciaran Cronin. Cambridge, MA: MIT Press, 1993.

———. *Knowledge and Human Interest.* Translated by Jeremy Shapiro. Boston: Beacon Press, 1971.

———. *Legitimation Crisis.* Translated by Thomas McCarthy. Boston: Beacon Press, 1971.

———. *Moral Consciousness and Communicative Action.* Translated by Christian Lenhardt and Shierry Weber Nicholsen. Cambridge, MA: MIT Press, 1990.

———. *On the Pragmatics of Communication.* Translated by B. Fultner. Cambridge, MA: MIT Press, 1998.

———. *The Philosophical Discourse of Modernity: Twelve Letters.* Translated by Frederick Lawrence. Cambridge, MA: MIT Press, 1987.

———. *Postmetaphysical Thinking.* Translated by William Mark Hohengarten. Cambridge, MA: MIT Press, 1992.

————. *The Postnational Constellation.* Translated and edited by M. Pensky. Cambridge, MA: MIT Press, 2001.

————. *Religion and Rationality: Essays on Reason, God, and Modernity.* Edited by E. Medieta. Cambridge, MA: MIT Press, 2002.

————. "Religion in the Public Sphere." Translated by J. Gaines. In *European Journal of Philosophy* 14 (2006): 1–25.

————. *The Structural Transformation of the Public Sphere.* Translated by T. Burger and F. Lawrence. Cambridge, MA: MIT Press, 1989.

————. *Theorie des Kommunikativen Handelns.* Frankfurt am Main: Suhrkamp, 1987. Translated by Thomas McCarthy as *The Theory of Communicative Action.* 2 Vols. Boston: Beacon Press, 1984, 1987.

————. *Theory and Practice.* Translated by John Viertel. Boston: Beacon Press, 1973.

————. *Truth and Justification.* Edited and Translated by Barbara Fultner. Cambridge, MA: MIT Press, 2003.

Habermas, Jürgen, and Joseph Ratzinger. *The Dialectics of Secularization: On Reason and Religion.* Translated by B. McNeil. San Francisco: Ignatius, 2006.

Hahn, Lewis Edwin. *Perspectives on Habermas.* Chicago: Open Court, 2000.

Haight, Roger. *The Christian Community in History.* Vol. 2, *Comparative Ecclesiology.* New York: Continuum, 2005.

Heath, Joseph. *Communicative Action and Rational Choice.* Cambridge, MA: MIT Press, 2001.

Held, David. *Introduction to Critical Theory: Horkheimer to Habermas.* Berkeley: University of California Press, 1980.

Held, David, and Anthony McCrew, eds. *The Global Transformations Reader.* Cambridge: Polity Press, 2000.

Horgen, Thaddeus, ed. *Walking Together: Roman Catholics and Ecumenism Twenty-Five Years after Vatican II.* Grand Rapids, MI: Eerdmans, 1990.

Hollenweger, W., and G. Pulkington. "Unity in the Spirit: Can It Be a Substitute for Organic Church Union?" *Church Times* 5788 (1974): 11–15.

John Paul II. *Ut Unam Sint.* Encyclical Letter by the Supreme Pontiff John Paul II on Commitment to Ecumenism. Translated by the United States Conference of Catholic Bishops. Washington, DC: United States Conference of Catholic Bishops, 1995.

Johnson, David Enderton, ed. *Uppsala to Nairobi 1968–1975: Report of the Central Committee to the Fifth Assembly of the World Council of Churches.* London: SPCK, 1975.

Jones, E. Stanley. "Is Federal Union Organic Union?" *Christian Century* 5 (February 1, 1950): 138–40.

Jungkuntz, R. "Lutheran Quest for a More Visible Unity." *Christianity Today* 13, (1969): 5–6.

Kasper, Walter. *That They May All Be One: The Call to Unity Today.* New York: Continuum / Barnes and Oates, 2004.

Kennion, R. W. *Unity and Order, the Handmaids of Truth: An Inquiry into God's Will and Our Duty Concerning the Unity and Order of the Visible Church with Special Reference to the Church of England and Those Who Dissent from It.* London: Seely, 1892.

Kinnamon, Michael, ed. *Towards Visible Unity: Commission on Faith and Order, Lima 1982.* Vol. 2, *Study Papers and Reports.* Geneva: WCC, 1982.

————. *The Vision of the Ecumenical Movement and How It Has Been Impoverished by Its Friends.* St. Louis, MO: Chalice Press, 2003.

Kinnamon, Michael, and Brian Cope, eds. *The Ecumenical Movement: An Anthology of Key Texts and Voices.* Geneva: WCC, 1997.

Lane, C. R. *Thoughts on the Unity of the Visible Church, and the Re-Union of the Churches.* Philadelphia: Reformed Church Publication Board, 1887.

Lara, Maria Pia. *Moral Textures: Feminist Discourse in the Public Sphere.* Berkeley: University of California Press, 1999.

Limouris, Gennadios, ed. *Orthodox Visions of Ecumenism: Statements, Messages and Reports on the Ecumenical Movement, 1902–1992.* Geneva: WCC, 1994.

Lodberg, Peter. "Common Understanding and Vision: An Analysis of the Responses to the Process." *The Ecumenical Review* 50, no. 3 (July 1998): 268–77.

Love, Janice. "Doing Democracy Differently: The Special Commission on Orthodox Participation in the WCC." *The Ecumenical Review* 55, no.1 (January 2003): 72–75.

Lossky, Nicholas, et al., eds. *Dictionary of the Ecumenical Movement.* 2nd ed. Geneva: WCC, 2002.

Lynch, Joseph. *The Medieval Church: A Brief History.* London and New York: Longman, 1992.

Macquarrie, J. "Is Organic Union Desirable?" *Theology* 73 (October 1970): 437–44.

Mathews, Matthew. "The Persistence of Religious Meaning in the Critical Theory of Jürgen Habermas." *Soundings* 82 (1999): 383–99.

McBrien, Richard. *Catholicism.* Revised edition. New York: HarperCollins, 1994.

McCarthy, Thomas. *The Critical Theory of Jürgen Habermas.* Cambridge, MA: MIT Press, 1978.

————. *Ideals and Illusions.* Cambridge, MA: MIT Press, 1991.

————. "Reflections on Rationalization in the Theory of Communicative Action." In R. J. Bernstein, ed., *Habermas and Modernity.* Cambridge: Polity Press, 1985.

McCaughey, Davis. *Piecing Together a Shared Vision.* Crows Nest: Australian Broadcasting Corporation, 1988.

Meehan, Johanna, ed. *Feminists Read Habermas: Gendering the Subject of Discourse.* New York: Routledge, 1995.

Mendieta, Eduardo, ed. *The Frankfurt School on Religion: Key Writings by the Major Thinkers.* New York: Routledge, 2005.

Meyendorff, John. *The Orthodox Church: Its Past and Its Role in the World Today.* New York: St. Vladimir's Seminary Press, 1981.

Meyer, Harding. "Christian World Communions: Identity and Ecumenical Calling." *The Ecumenical Review* 46, no. 4 (October 1994): 383–93.

―――. *That All May Be One: Perceptions and Models of Ecumenicity.* Grand Rapids, MI: Eerdmans, 1999.

Meyer, Harding, and Lukas Vischer, eds. *Growth in Agreement: Reports and Agreed Statements of Ecumenical Conversation on a World Level.* Geneva: WCC, 1984.

Morris, J., and N. Sagovsky. *The Unity We Have and the Unity We Seek: Ecumenical Prospects for the Third Millennium.* London: T&T Clark, 2003.

Müller-Doohm, Stefan, ed. *Das Interesse der Vernunft: Rückblicke auf das Werk von Jürgen Habermas seit Erkenntnis und Interesse."* Frankfurt am Main: Suhrkamp, 2000.

Newbigin, Bishop. "Comments on 'The Church, the Churches and the World Council of Churches.'" *The Ecumenical Review* 3, no. 3 (April 1951): 252–54.

Oakley, Francis. *Council over Pope: Toward a Provisional Ecclesiology.* New York: Herder and Herder, 1969.

O'Malley, John. *Tradition and Transition: Historical Perspectives on Vatican II.* Lima, OH: Academic Renewal Press, 2002.

Otte, Hans, and Richard Schenk, eds. "Eine Oekumene des Einspruchs. Systematische Ueberlegungen zum heutigen oekumenischen Prozess aus einer roemisch-katholischen Sicht." In *Die Reunionsgespraeche im Niedersachsen des 17. Jahrhunderts. Rojas y Spinola—Molan—Leibniz.* Goettingen: Vandenhoeck & Ruprecht, 1999.

Payne, Ernest. "Working Out the New Delhi Statement on Unity." *The Ecumenical Review* 14, no. 3 (April 1962): 296–305.

Pius XI. *Mortalium Animos.* Translated by Rev. R. McGowan. Washington, DC: National Catholic Welfare Conference, 1928.

Raiser, Konrad. *Ecumenism in Transition: A Paradigm Shift in the Ecumenical Movement?* Geneva: WCC, 1991.

―――. "Universal Council, Goal of the Ecumenical Movement?" *Reformed World* 32, no. 5 (March 1971): 202–10.

Rahner, Karl. "Towards a Fundamental Theological Interpretation of Vatican II." *Theological Studies* 40, no.4 (December 1979): 716–27.

Rehg, William. "Discourse Ethics." In E. Wyschogrod and G. P. McKenny, eds., *The Ethical*, 83–100. Malden, MA; Blackwell, 2003.

―――. "Discourse Ethics and Individual Conscience." In N. Gottschalk-Mazouz, ed., *Perspektiven der Diskursethik*, 26–40. Würzburg: Königshausen and Neumann, 2004.

―――. "Reason and Rhetoric in Habermas's Theory of Argumentation." In W. Jost and M. J. Hyde, eds., *Rhetoric and Hermeneutics in Our Time*, 358–77. New Haven, CT: Yale University Press, 1997.

Representatives of the Presbyterian Church of England and the Congregational Union of England and Wales, appointed to consider the possibilities of organic union. Joint Conference Report. London: Independent Press, 1948.

Rhodes, M. J. *The Visible Unity of the Catholic Church Maintained against Opposite Theories: With an Explanation of Certain Passages in Ecclesiastical History, Erroneously Appealed to in Their Support Place*. London: Longmans, Green and Co., 1870.

Richards, George W. "The Historical Significance of Denominationalism," a Paper Read before the Conference on Organic Union Held at the Invitation of the General Assembly of the Presbyterian Church in the USA, Witherspoon Building, Philadelphia, December 4–5, 1918. Philadelphia: Publication Committee of the Conference on Organic Union, 1918.

Rodger, R. C. "Organic Church Union: Are Churchmen Ready? Yes, Spiritual Unity Cannot Exist without Organic Church Union." *Christianity Today* 10 (November 5, 1965): 4.

Roman Catholic–Lutheran Joint Commission. *Facing Unity: Models, Forms and Phases of Catholic-Lutheran Church Fellowship*. Geneva: Lutheran World Federation, 1985.

Ross, J. M. *Visible Unity—What Does the Bible Say?* Littlehampton, Sussex: Friends of Reunion, 1963.

Rouse, Ruth, and Stephen Neill, eds. *A History of the Ecumenical Movement 1517–1968*. 3rd ed. Geneva: WCC, 1986.

Rush, Ormond. *Still Interpreting Vatican II: Some Hermeneutical Principles*. New York: Paulist Press, 2004.

Russell, Letty. *Church in the Round: Feminist Interpretation of the Church*. Louisville: Westminster John Knox Press, 1993.

Sacks, Jonathan. *The Dignity of Difference: How to Avoid the Clash of Civilizations*. New York: Continuum, 2002.

Schomberg, René vom, and Kenneth Baynes, eds. *Discourse and Democracy: Essays on Habermas's 'Between Facts and Norms.'* Albany, NY: SUNY Press, 2002.

Schreiter, Robert. *The New Catholicity: Theology between the Global and Local*. Maryknoll, NY: Orbis, 1997.

Schutz, Roger. "L'Unité Visible, Condition de Notre Présence." *Choisir* 135 (1971): 14.

Secretariat for the Promotion of Unity of Christians. *Ad totam ecclesiam*. Directory Concerning Ecumenical Matters, Part One. *Origins* 23 (July 29, 1993): 129.

Spivak, Gayatri. "Can the Subaltern Speak?" In Patrick Williams and Laura Chrisman, eds., *Colonial Discourse and Post-Colonial Theory: A Reader*, 66–111. New York: Columbia University Press, 1994

Stransky, Thomas. "Roman Catholic Membership in the World Council of Churches?" *The Ecumenical Review* 20, no. 3 (July 1968): 205–44.

Swindells, P. J. "Is Organic Union Desirable?" *Theology* 74 (1971): 28–31.

Tanner, Mary. "Towards a Common Understanding and Vision: A Faith and Order Perspective." *The Ecumenical Review* 50, no. 3 (July 1998): 357–66.

Taylor, Charles. *A Secular Age*. Cambridge, MA: Harvard University Press, 2007.

Thompson, David. "Visible Unity as Gift and Call: A Reaction to the Canberra Unity Statement from the Perspective of the United and Uniting Churches." *The Ecumenical Review* 45, no. 1 (1993): 72–77.

Thompson, John, and David Held, eds. *Habermas: Critical Debates.* Cambridge, MA: MIT Press, 1982.

Thurian, Max, ed. *Churches Respond to BEM.* 6 Vols. Geneva: WCC, 1986.

———. *Visible Unity and Tradition.* London: Darton, Longman and Todd, 1964.

———. "The Visible Unity of Christians." *The Ecumenical Review* 13, no. 3 (April 1961): 313–34.

Tierney, Brian. *Foundations of the Conciliar Theory: The Contribution of the Medieval Canonists from Gratian to the Great Schism.* Cambridge: Cambridge University Press, 1955.

Tillard, Jean-Marie Roger. *Church of Churches: The Ecclesiology of Communion.* Collegeville, MN: Liturgical Press, 1992.

Tjørhom, Ola. "The Goal of Visible Unity: Reaffirming Our Commitment." *The Ecumenical Review* 54, nos. 1–2 (2002): 162–71.

———.*Visible Church—Visible Unity: Ecumenical Ecclesiology and "The Great Tradition of the Church."* Foreword by Geoffrey Wainwright. Collegeville, MN: Liturgical Press, 2004.

Van der Bent, Ans Joachim. *Historical Dictionary of Ecumenical Christianity.* Metuchen NJ: Scarecrow, 1994.

———. *Six Hundred Ecumenical Consultations 1948–1982.* Geneva: WCC, 1983.

———. *Vital Ecumenical Concerns: Sixteen Documentary Surveys.* Gevena: WCC, 1986.

Van Elderen, Marlin ed. *From Canberra to Harare: An Illustrated Account of the Life of the World Council of Churches 1991–1998.* Geneva: WCC, 1998.

———. *Introducing the World Council of Churches.* Geneva: WCC, 2001.

Vischer, Lukas. *The Unity of the Church: A Report to the Central Committee, August 1973.* Translated from the German by the WCC language service. Geneva: WCC, 1973.

Visser 't Hooft, Willem A. *The Genesis and Formation of the World Council of Churches.* Geneva: WCC Publications, 1982.

———. "Various Meanings of Unity and the Unity Which the World Council of Churches Seeks to Promote." *The Ecumenical Review* 8, no. 1 (October 1955): 18–29.

———. "The World Council of Churches: Its Nature—Its Limits," (First Draft) Study 47E/102A, March 1947. Geneva: World Council of Churches Study Dept., 1947.

Vos, J. G. "The Unity of the Visible Church." *Reformation Review* 12, no. 3 (1964–65): 148–55.

Wainwright, Geoffrey. *The Ecumenical Movement: Crisis and Opportunity for the Church.* Grand Rapids, MI: Eerdmans, 1983.

White, Stephen, ed. *The Cambridge Companion to Habermas.* Cambridge: Cambridge University Press, 1995.

World Council of Churches Central Committee. *And So Set Up Signs . . . The World Council of Churches' First 40 Years*. Geneva: WCC, 1988.

————. "The Church, the Churches and the World Council of Churches: The Ecclesiological Significance of the World Council of Churches." In Lukas Vischer, ed., *A Documentary History of the Faith and Order Movement 1927–1963*. St. Louis, MO: Bethany Press, 1963.

————. *From Harare to Porto Alegre 1998–2006*. Geneva: WCC, 2005.

————. *Nairobi to Vancouver: 1975–1983, Report of the Central Committee to the Sixth Assembly of the World Council of Churches*. Geneva: WCC, 1983.

————. *Yearbook: World Council of Churches*. Annual vols. Geneva: WCC 1995–2003.

World Council of Churches Commission on Faith and Order. *Baptism, Eucharist and Ministry*. Geneva: WCC, 1982.

————. *Beyond Unity-in-Tension: Unity, Renewal and the Community of Women and Men*. Geneva: WCC, 1988.

————. *Living Today Towards Visible Unity*. Geneva: WCC, 1988.

————. *The Nature and Mission of the Church: A Stage on the Way to a Common Statement*. Geneva: WCC, 2005.

————. *On the Way to Fuller Koinonia: Official Report of the Fifth World Conference on Faith and Order*. Geneva: WCC, 1994.

————. "The Structure of Visible Unity: From a Report at the Faith and Order Conference, Nasrapur, India, August 1972." *National Christian Council Review* 92, no. 11 (1972): 464–68.

————. "Toward a Common Understanding and Vision of the World Council of Churches," in *Assembly Workbook for Harare 1998* (Geneva: WCC, 1998), 103.

————. *Unity and Renewal: A Study Guide for Local Groups; Program on the Unity of the Church and the Renewal of Human Community*. Geneva: World Council of Churches, 1987.

————. *Unity in Today's World: The Faith and Order Studies on "Unity of the Church—Unity of Humankind."* Geneva: WCC, 1978.

————. *The Unity of the Church: A Report to the Central Committee, August 1973*. Geneva: WCC, 1973.

————. *What Kind of Unity?* Faith and Order paper no. 69. Geneva: WCC, 1974.

————. *What Unity Requires*. Faith and Order paper no. 77. Geneva: WCC, 1976.

World Council of Churches General Assembly. *Breaking Barriers, Nairobi 1975: The Official Report of the Fifth Assembly of the World Council of Churches, Nairobi, 23 November–10 December, 1975*. Grand Rapids, MI: Eerdmans, 1976.

————. *The Evanston Report: The Second Assembly of the World Council of Churches, 1954*. New York: Harper and Brothers, 1955.

————. *The First Assembly of the World Council of Churches: The Official Report*. New York: Harper and Brothers, 1949.

————. *The New Delhi Report: The Third Assembly of the World Council of Churches, 1961*. London: SCM, 1961.

————. "Called to Be the One Church." *The Ecumenical Review* 58, nos. 1–2 (January–April 2006): 112–17.

————. *Official Report of the Seventh Assembly of the World Council of Churches, Canberra.* Geneva: WCC, 1991.

————. *Official Report of the Sixth Assembly of the World Council of Churches, Vancouver.* Geneva: WCC, 1983.

————. *Together on the Way: Official Report of the Eighth Assembly of the World Council of Churches, Harare.* Geneva: WCC, 1999.

————. *The Uppsala Report 1968: Official Report of the Fourth Assembly of the World Council of Churches.* Geneva: WCC, 1968.

World Lutheran Federation. *Communion—Visible Unity: Reports by Gunnar Staalsett, General Secretary, Lutheran World Federation, to Governing Bodies of the Lutheran World Federation, 1986–1991.* Geneva: Lutheran World Federation, 1991.

Zeno's Edict. Translated with commentary by A. Grillmeier in *Christ in Christian Tradition.* Vol. 2.1. Atlanta: John Knox Press, 1975.

Index